GOTHIC&FANTASY
HAND-DRAWN COLORING BOOK
By Emerian Rich

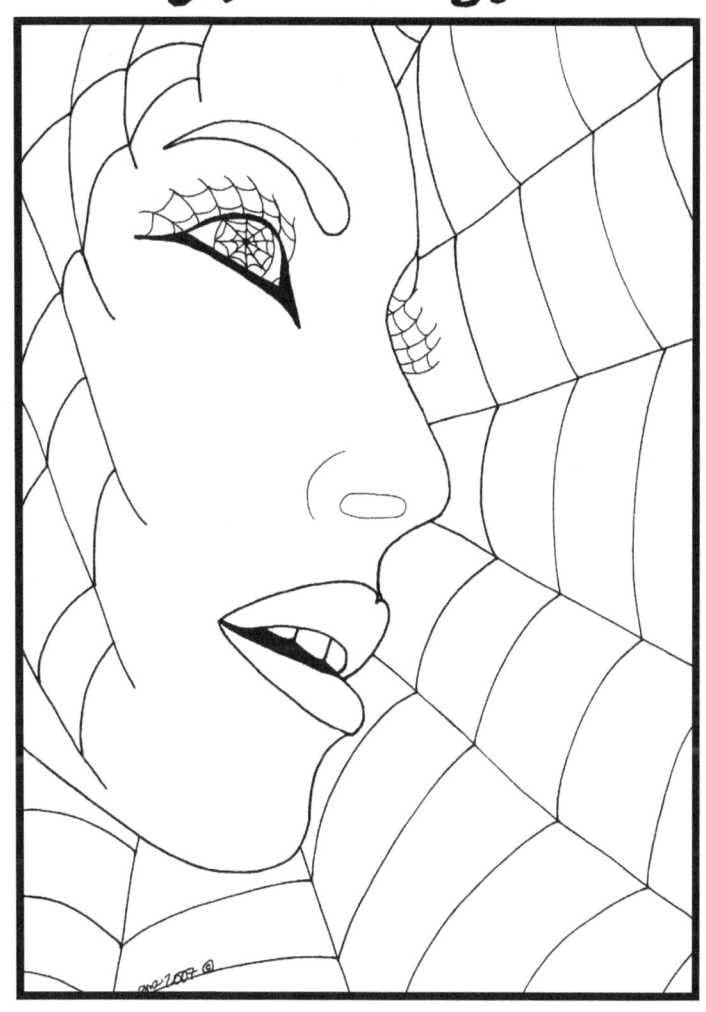

ART has always been a way for me to escape the stress and drama of real life and experience something out of the ordinary. From MC Escher's mind-blowing patterns, to the fun darkness of Edward Gorey, black and white art speaks to my soul. Our lives are composed of brilliant color and our minds are full of the moral, religious, and societal grays of belief. The absoluteness of black and white brings a calming sureness to my world. Black and white, good and evil, yin and yang, with no timidity or ambiguity. I hope these prints will both inspire you and allow you to relax by coloring your stresses away. ~Emz

ARTIST   Emerian Rich is an artist and writer with a degree in Visual Presentation and Space Design from FIDM. She writes mostly horror, and romance with a sprinkling of whatever else the mood strikes her. For more information on her work, check the back page, or go to emzbox.com.

DEDICATION   For all of my art patrons and admirers who asked me to make a coloring book, here it is finally! I hope you have fun coloring to your heart's content and I expect you to send me pictures. Enjoy.

ISBN-13: 978-1523792115
ISBN-10: 1523792116

Manufactured in the United States.
emzbox.com

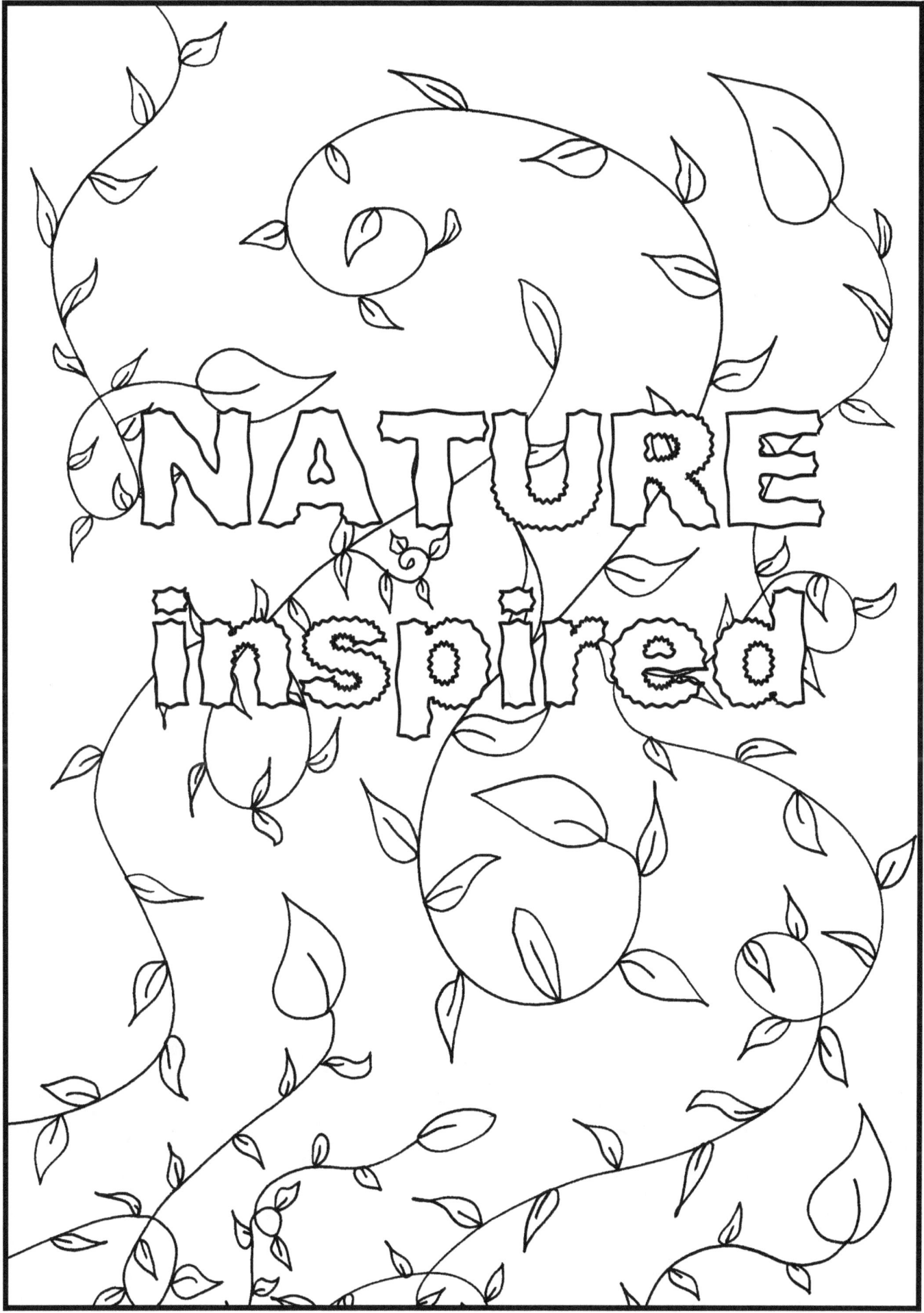

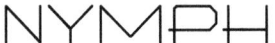
NYMPH

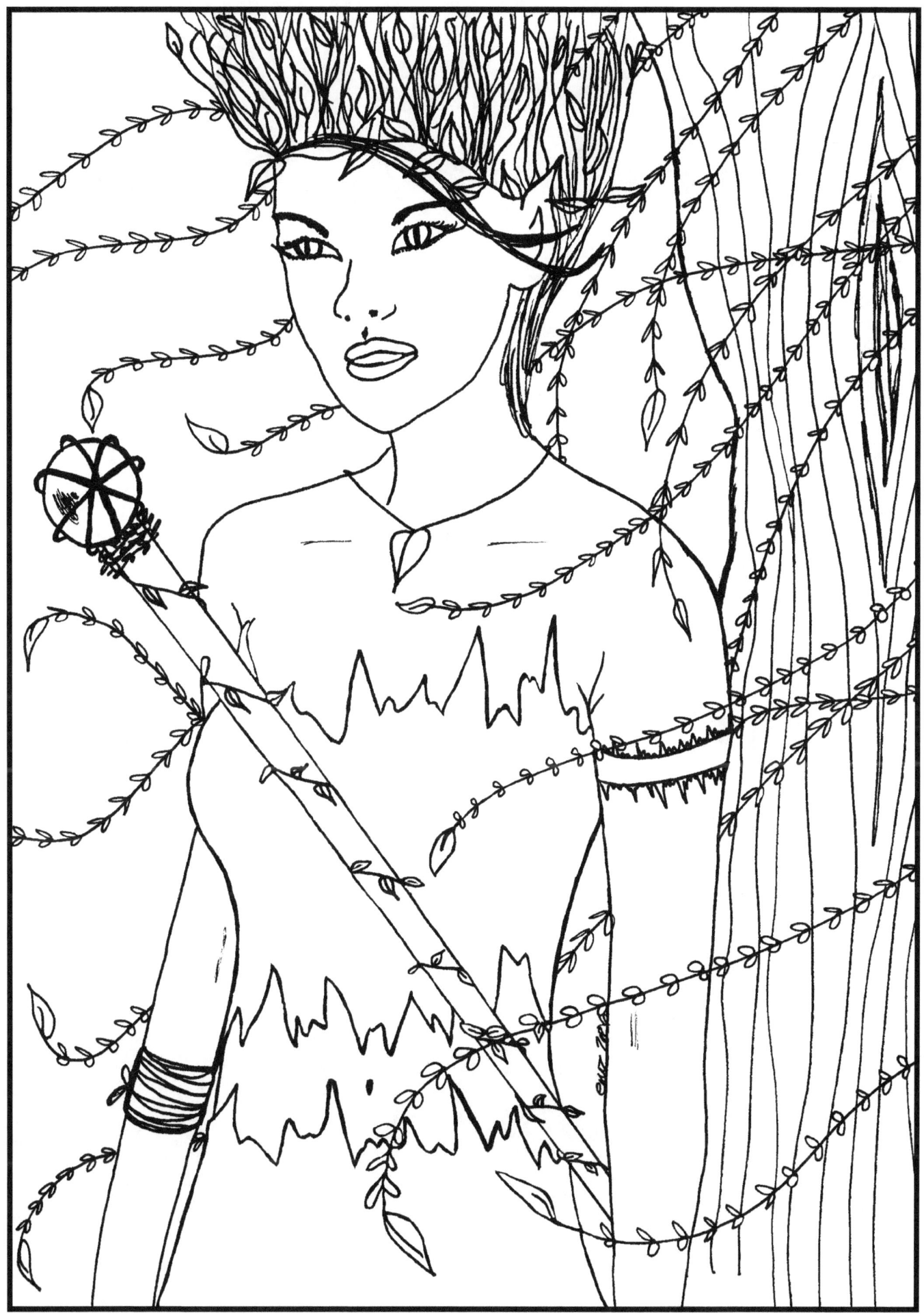

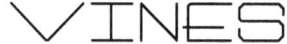

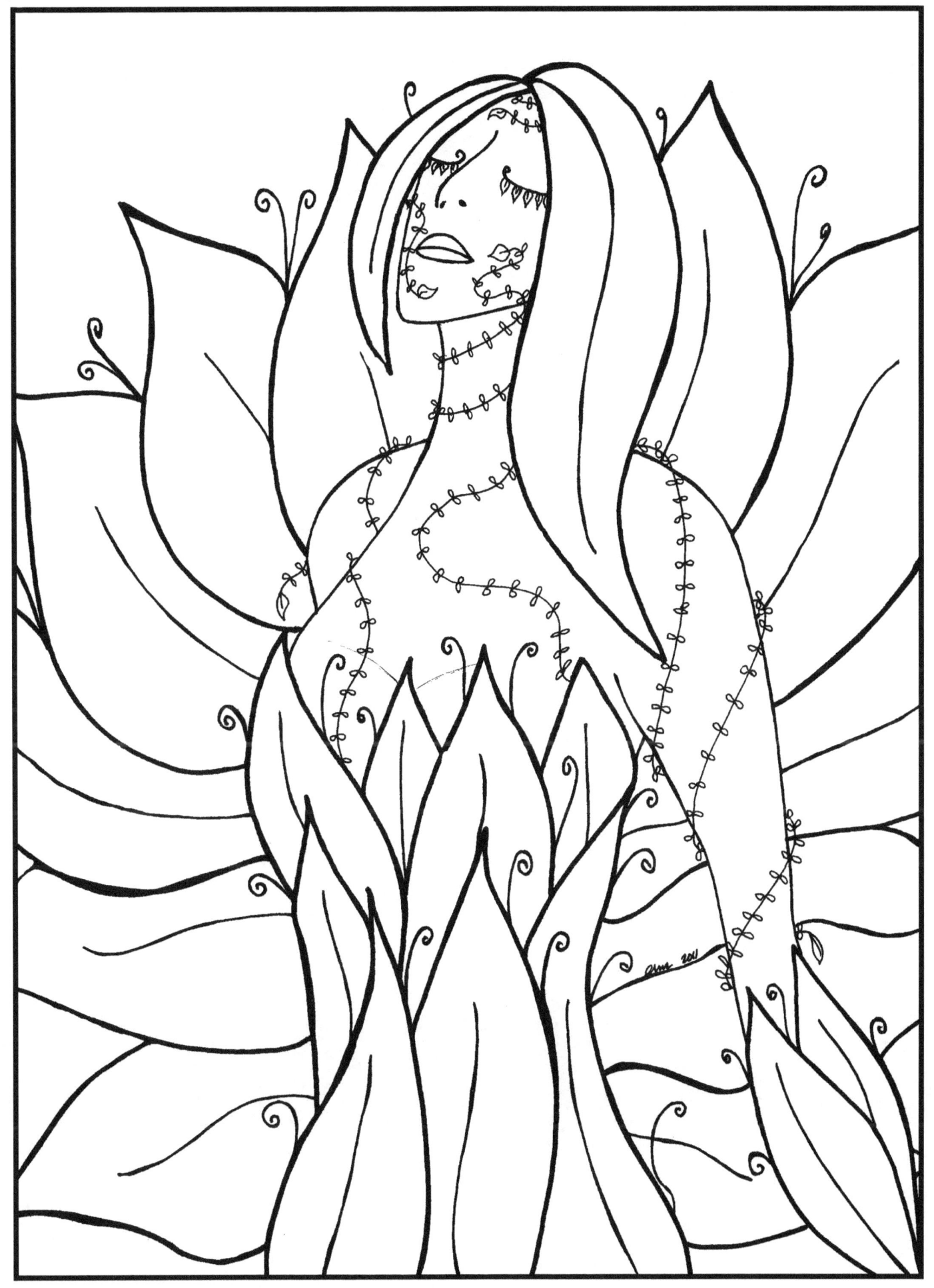

FLOWER BUD

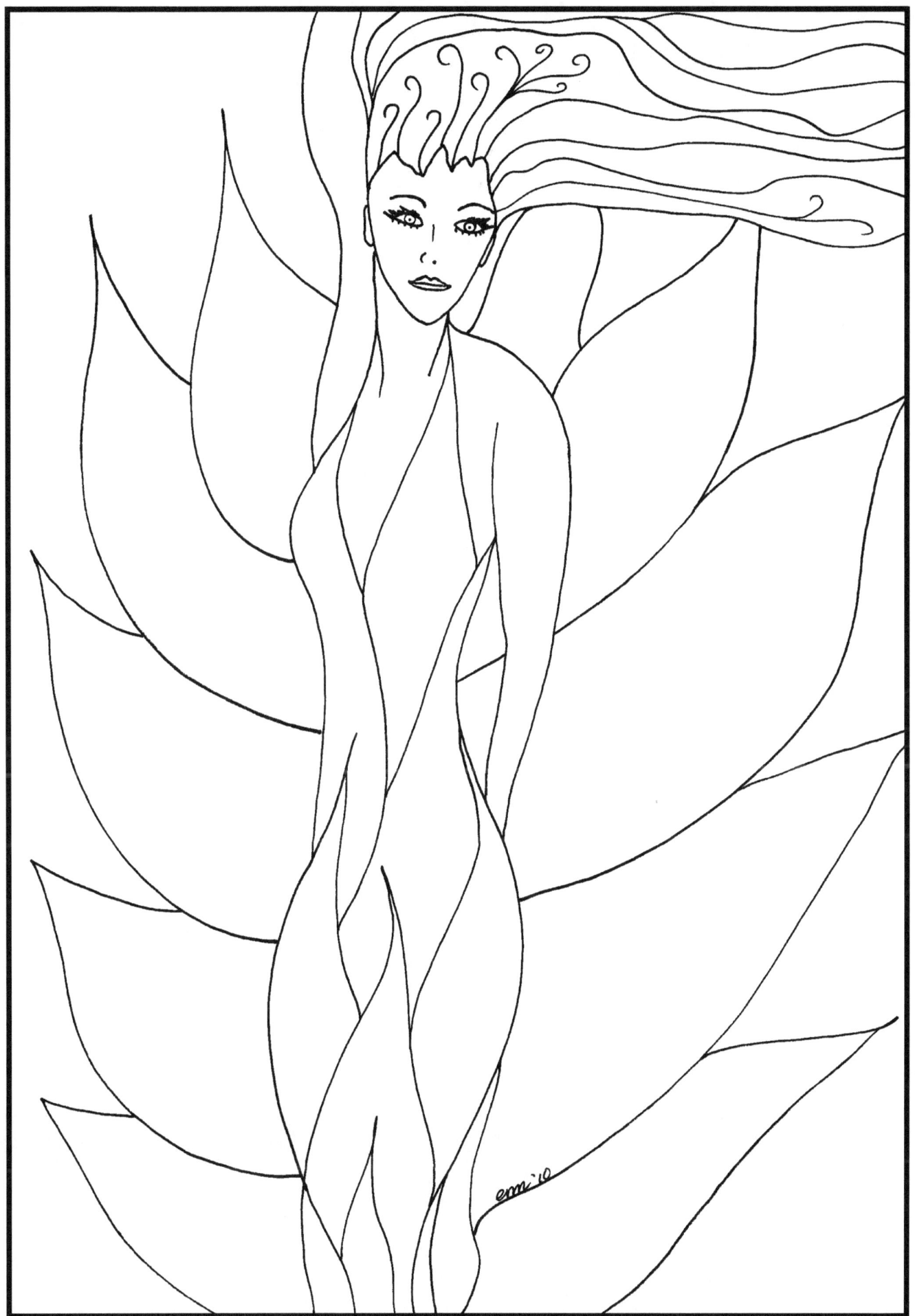

CASTING

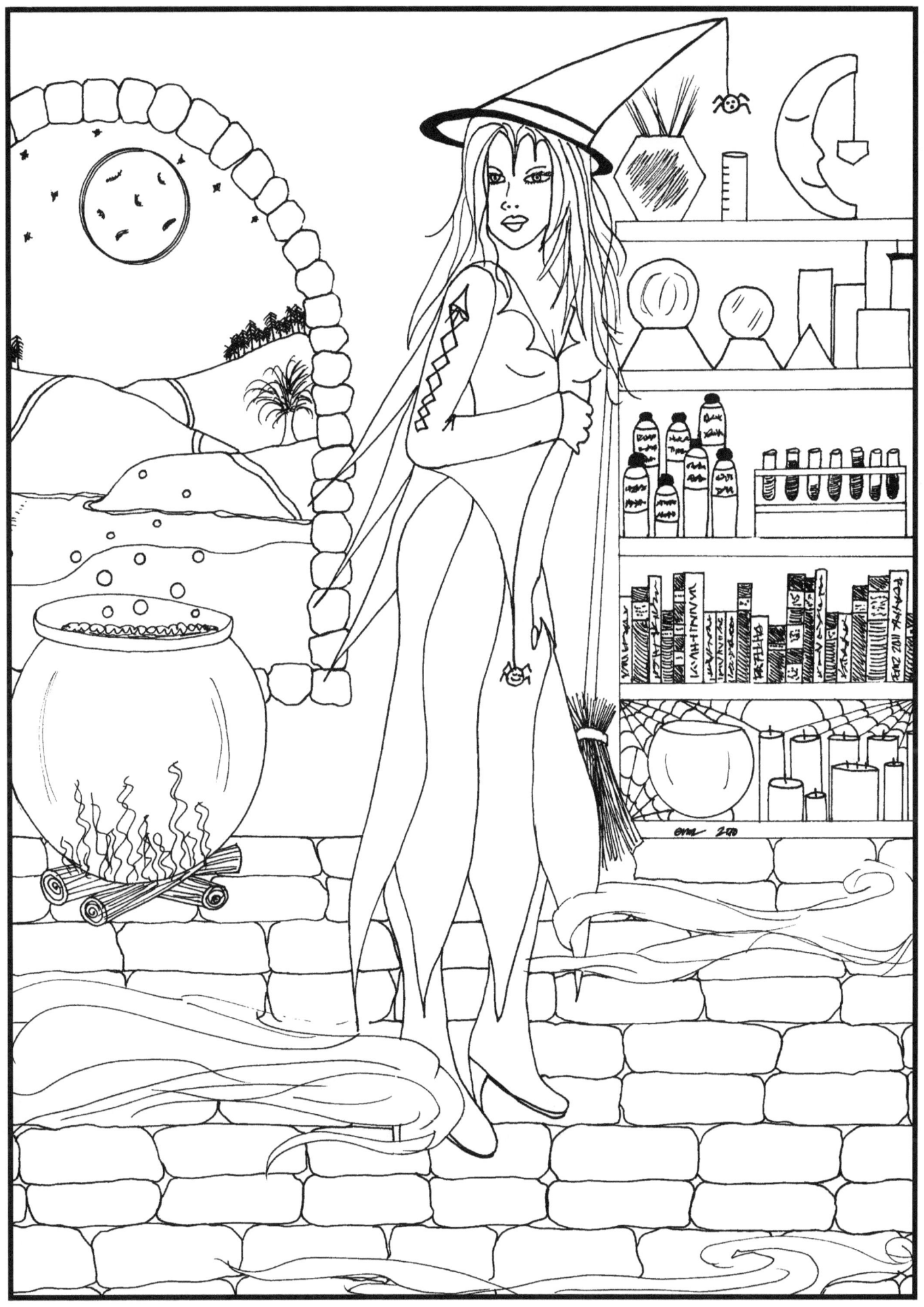

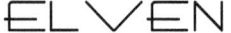

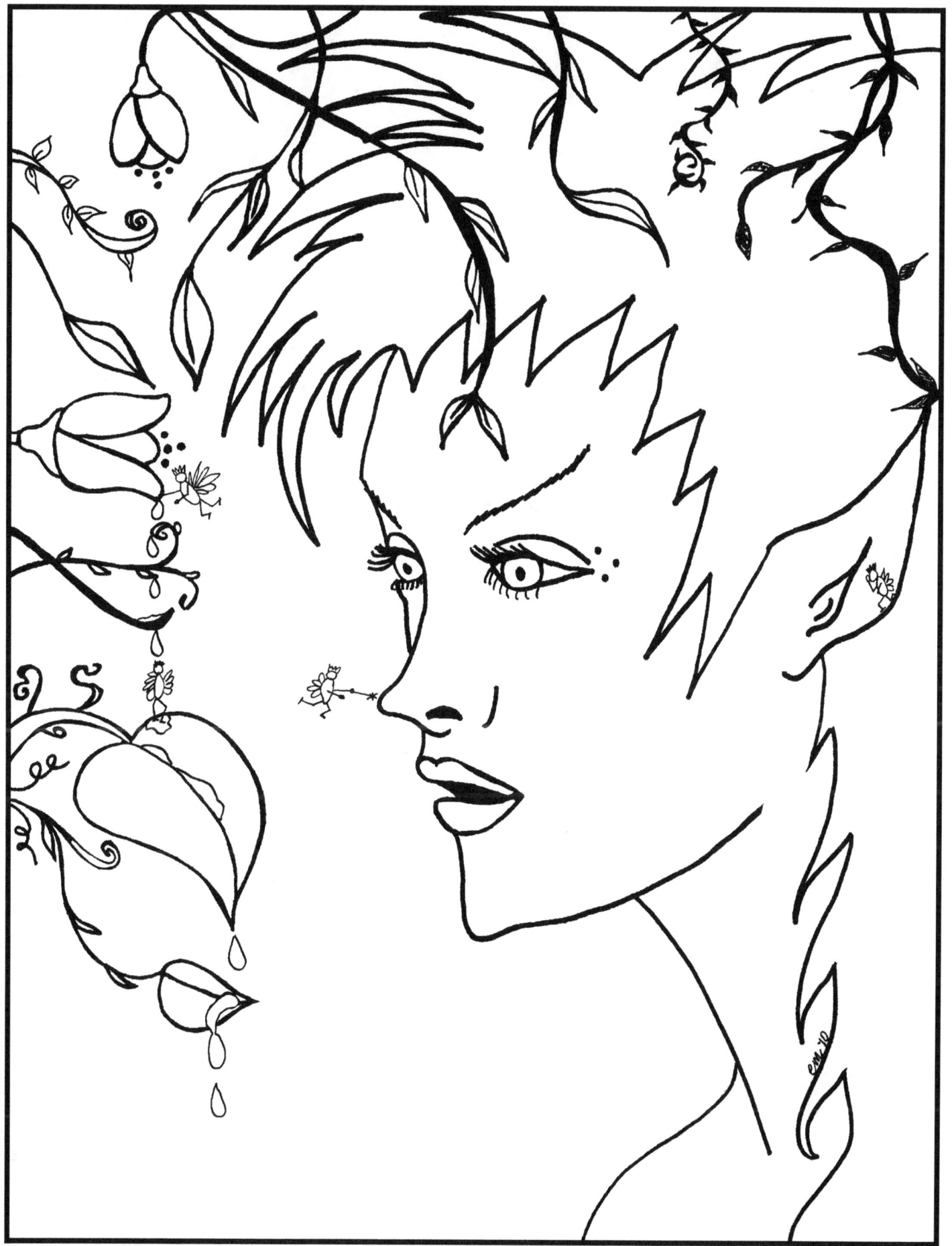

SPIDER LADY

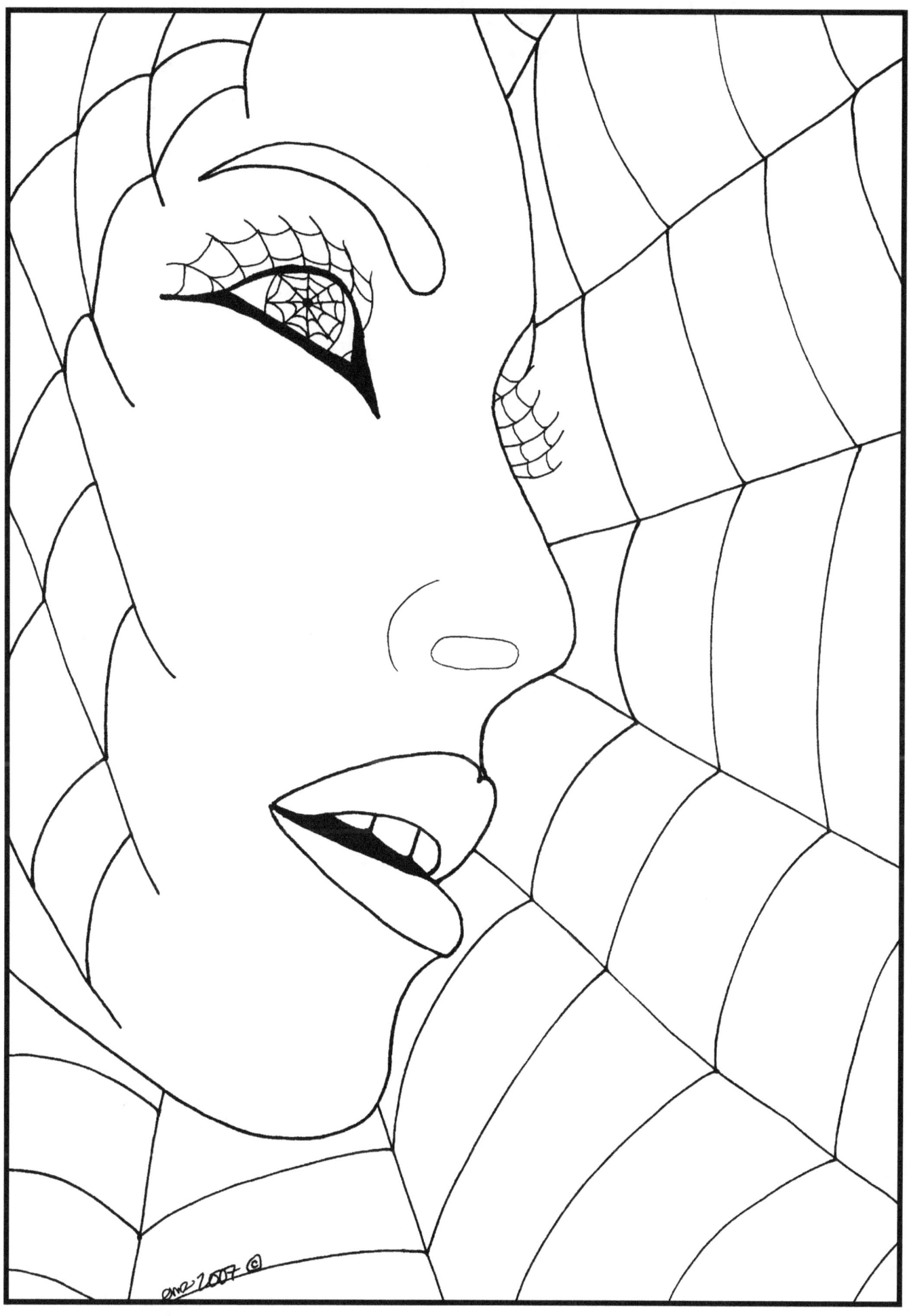

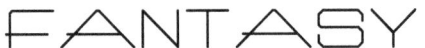

FANTASY

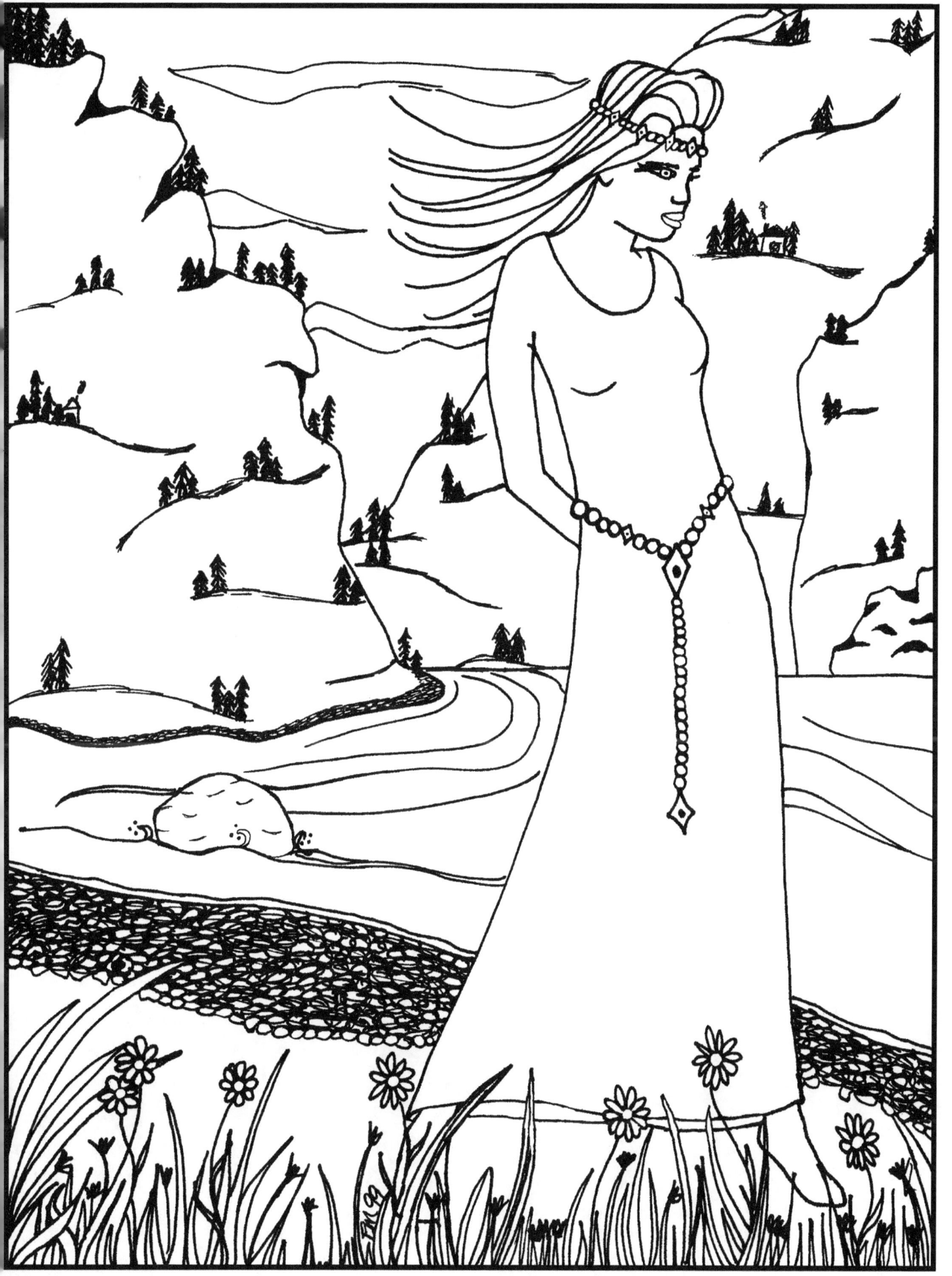

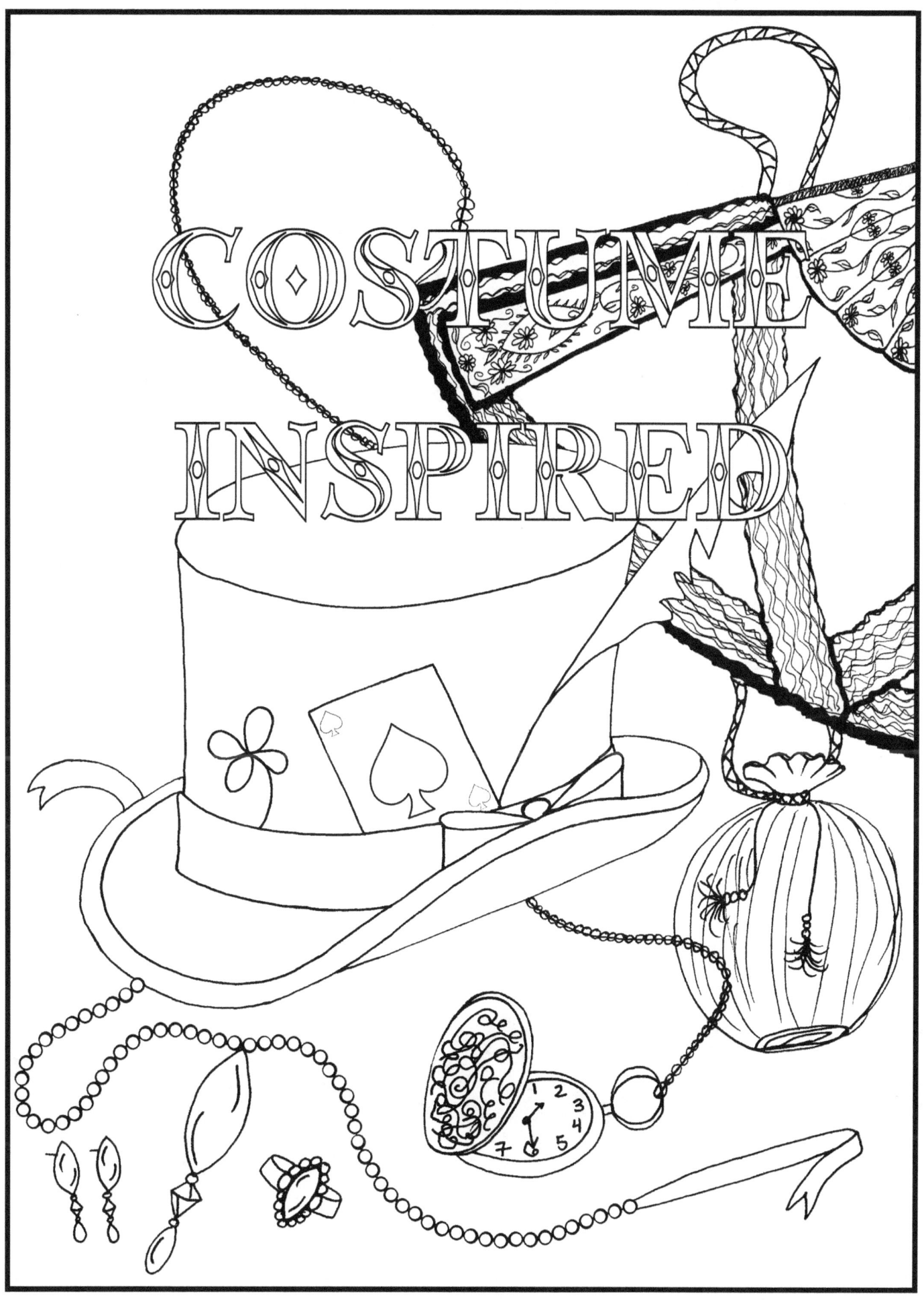

FAN GAL

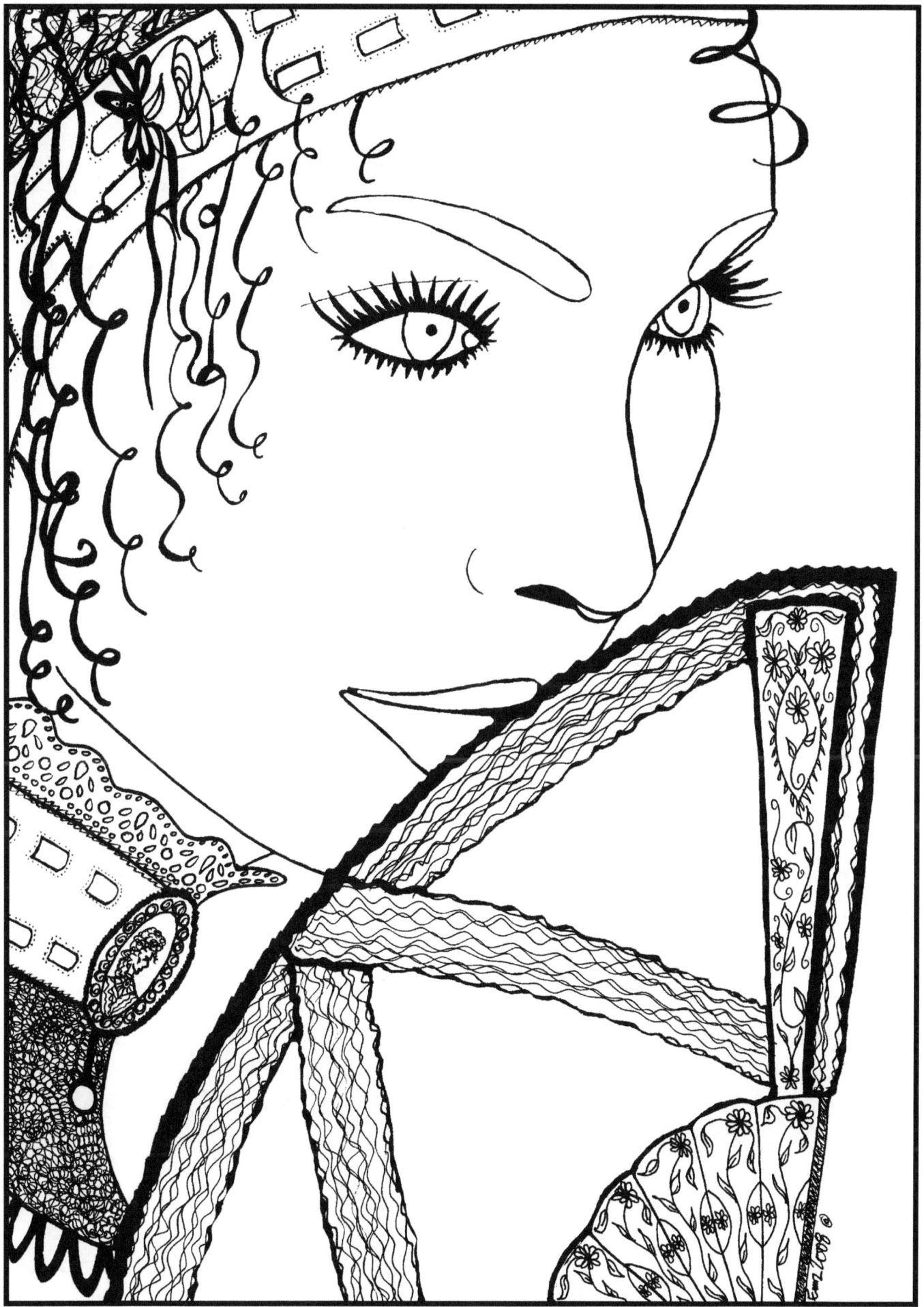

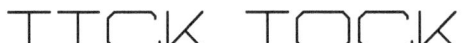

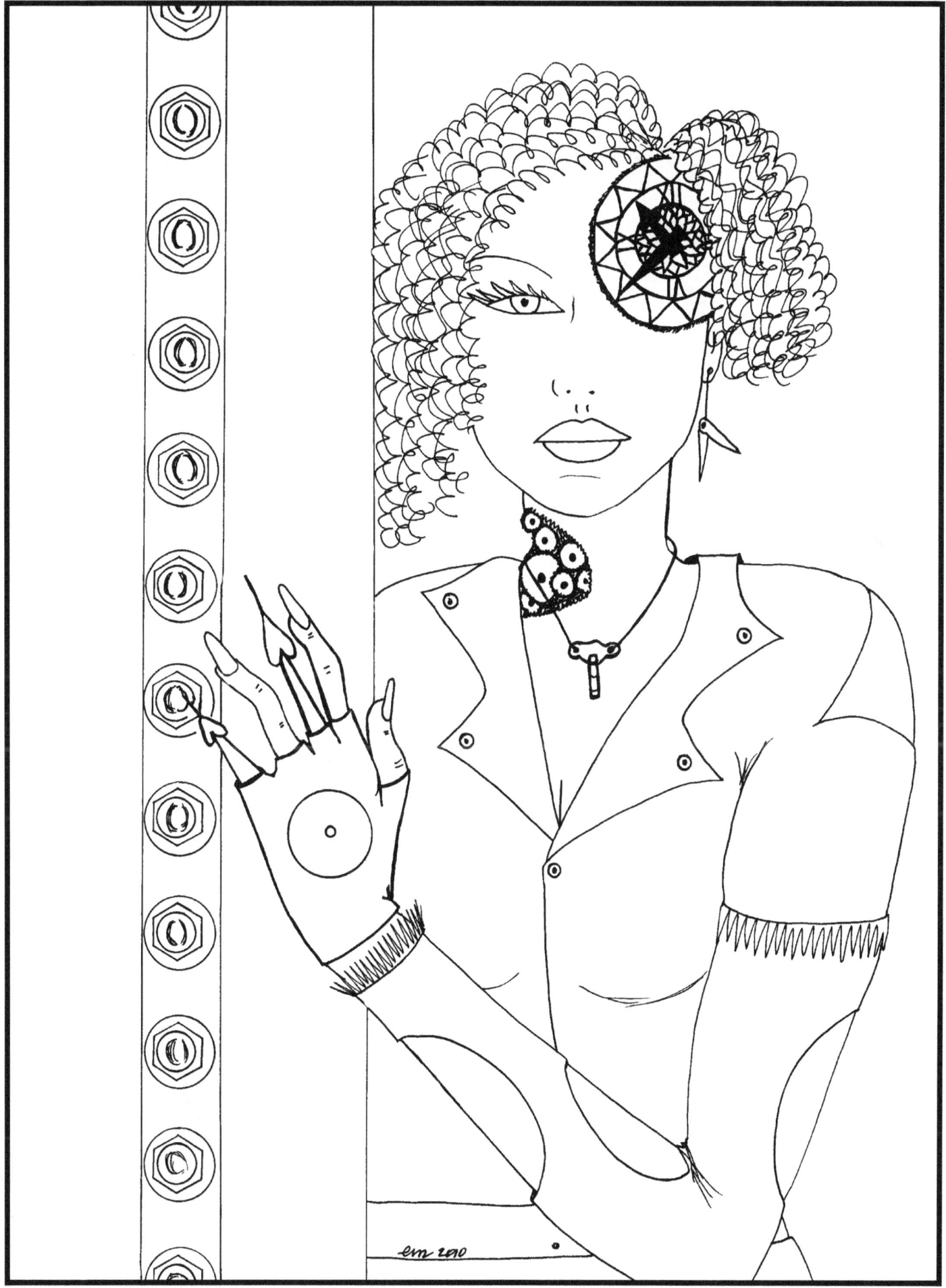

HOW DARE HE?

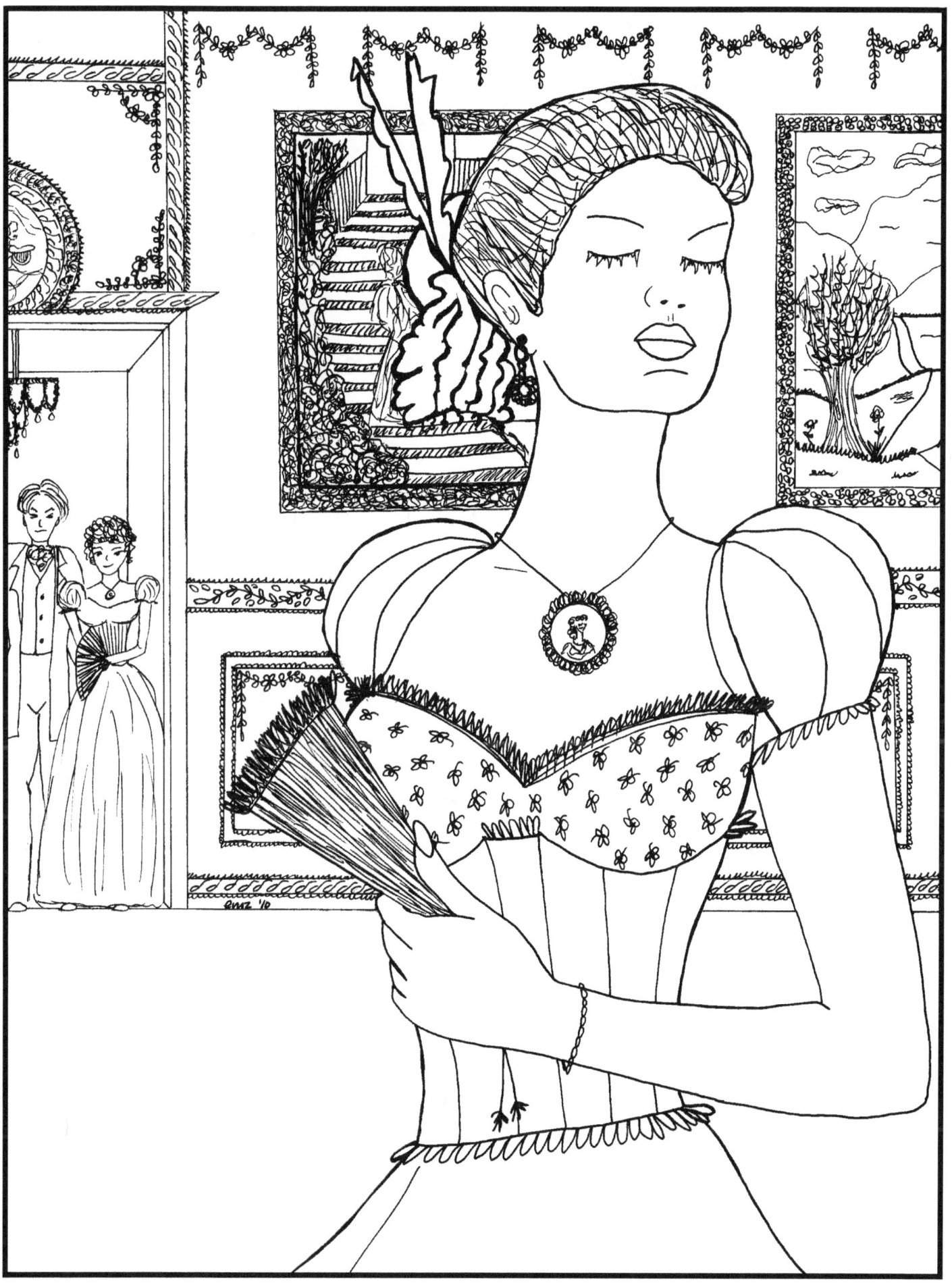

HEART LOLI

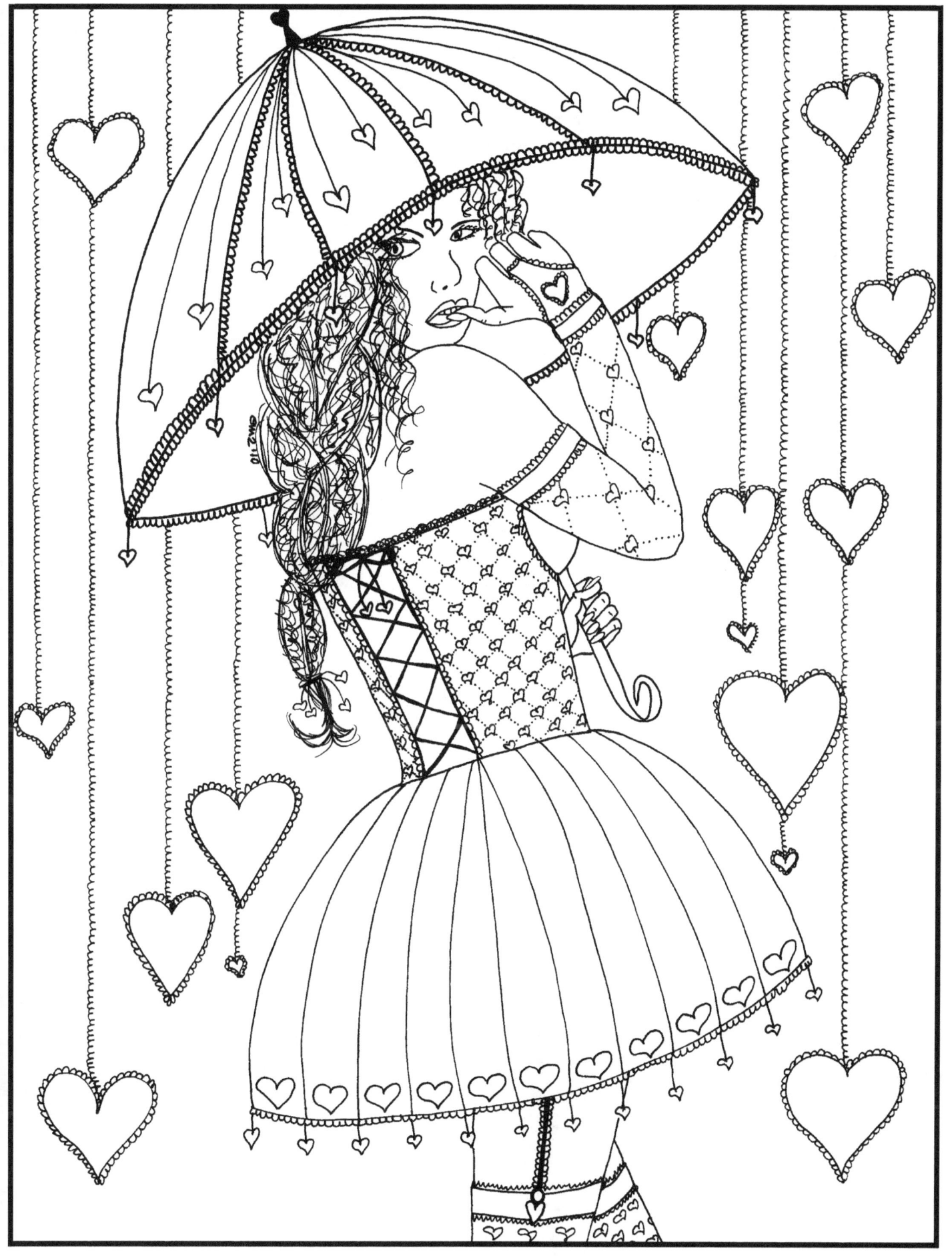

CYBER NURSE

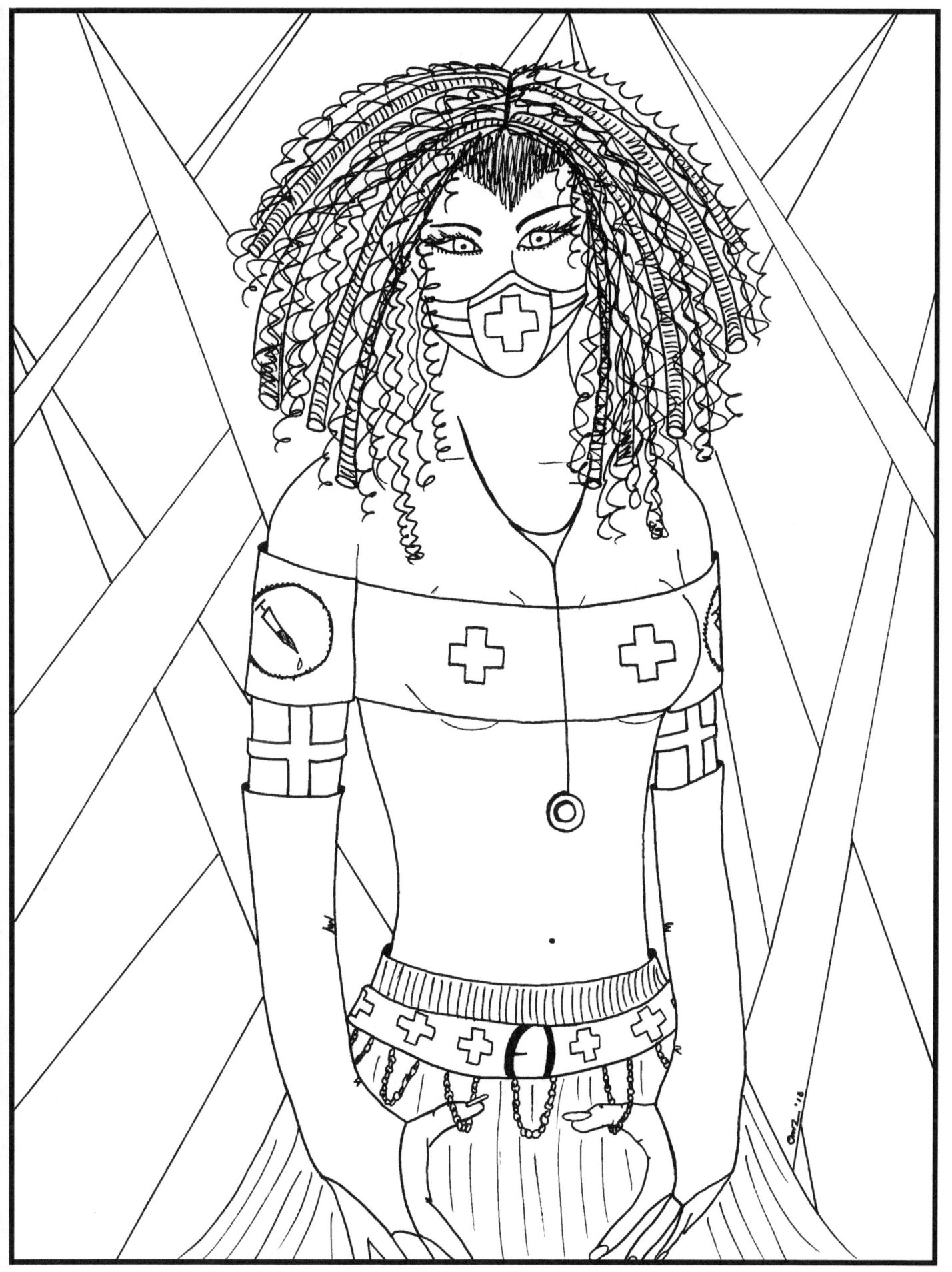

THOUGHT

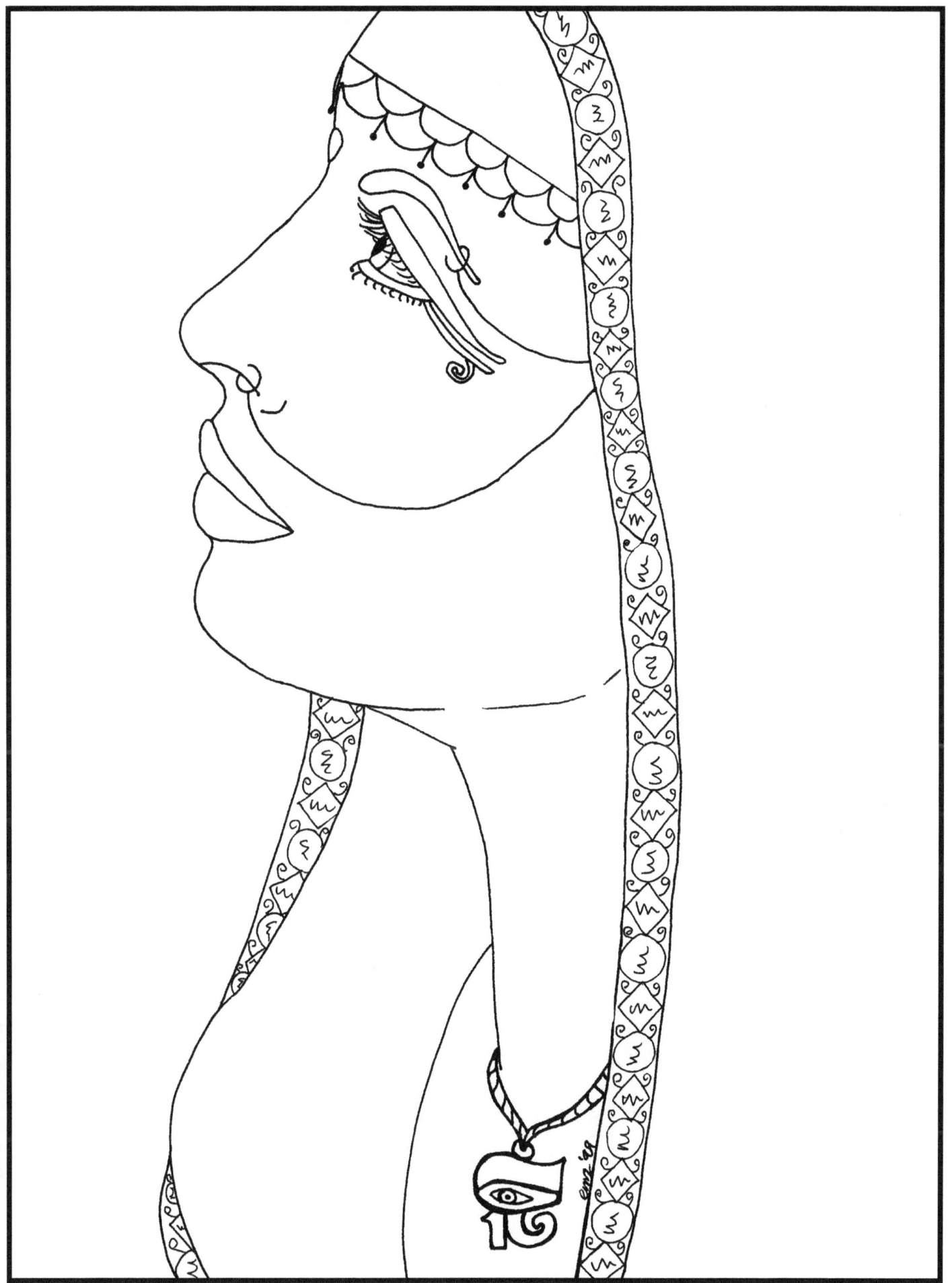

SPIDER COUTESS

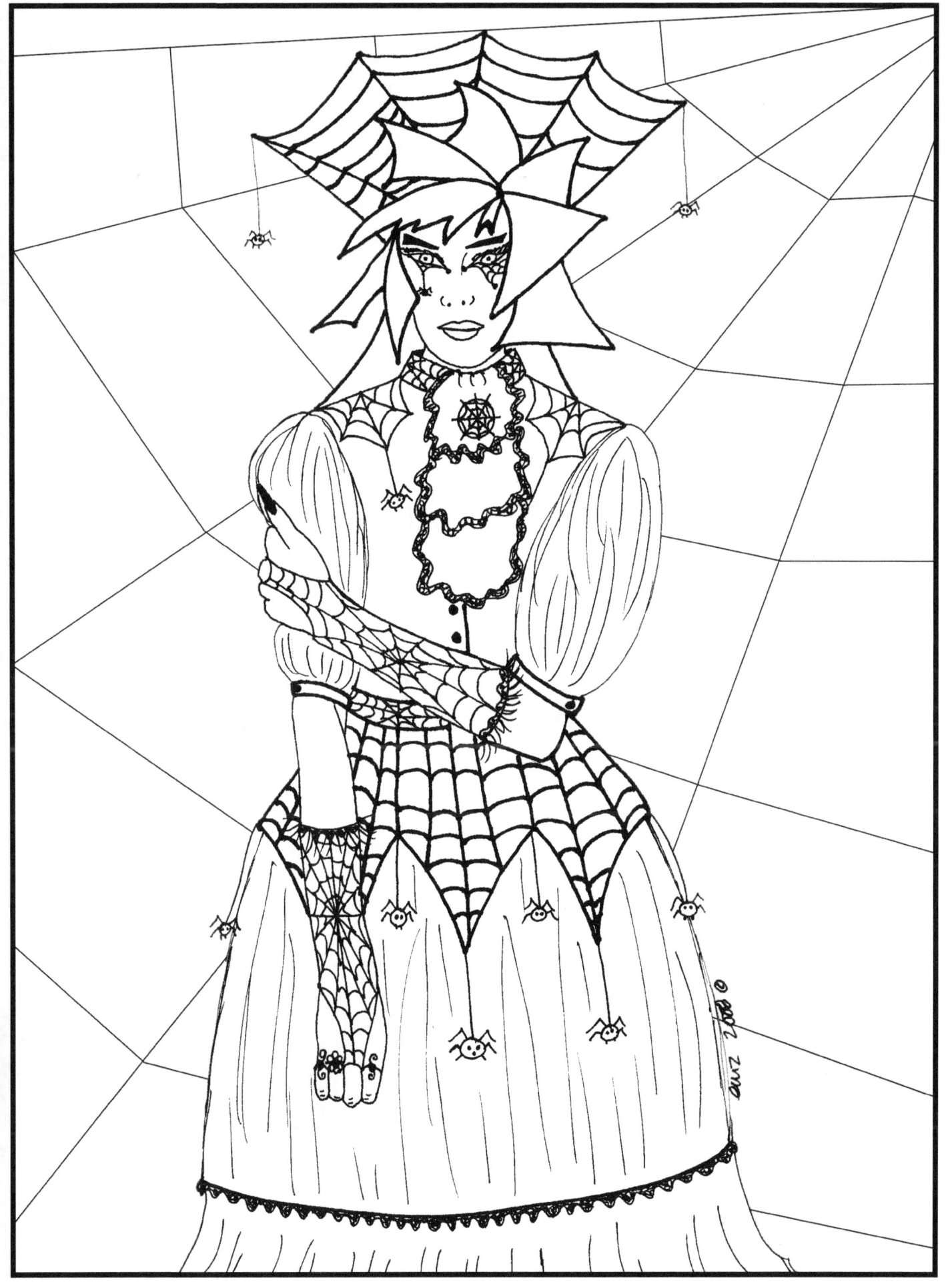

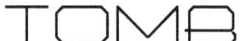

TOMB

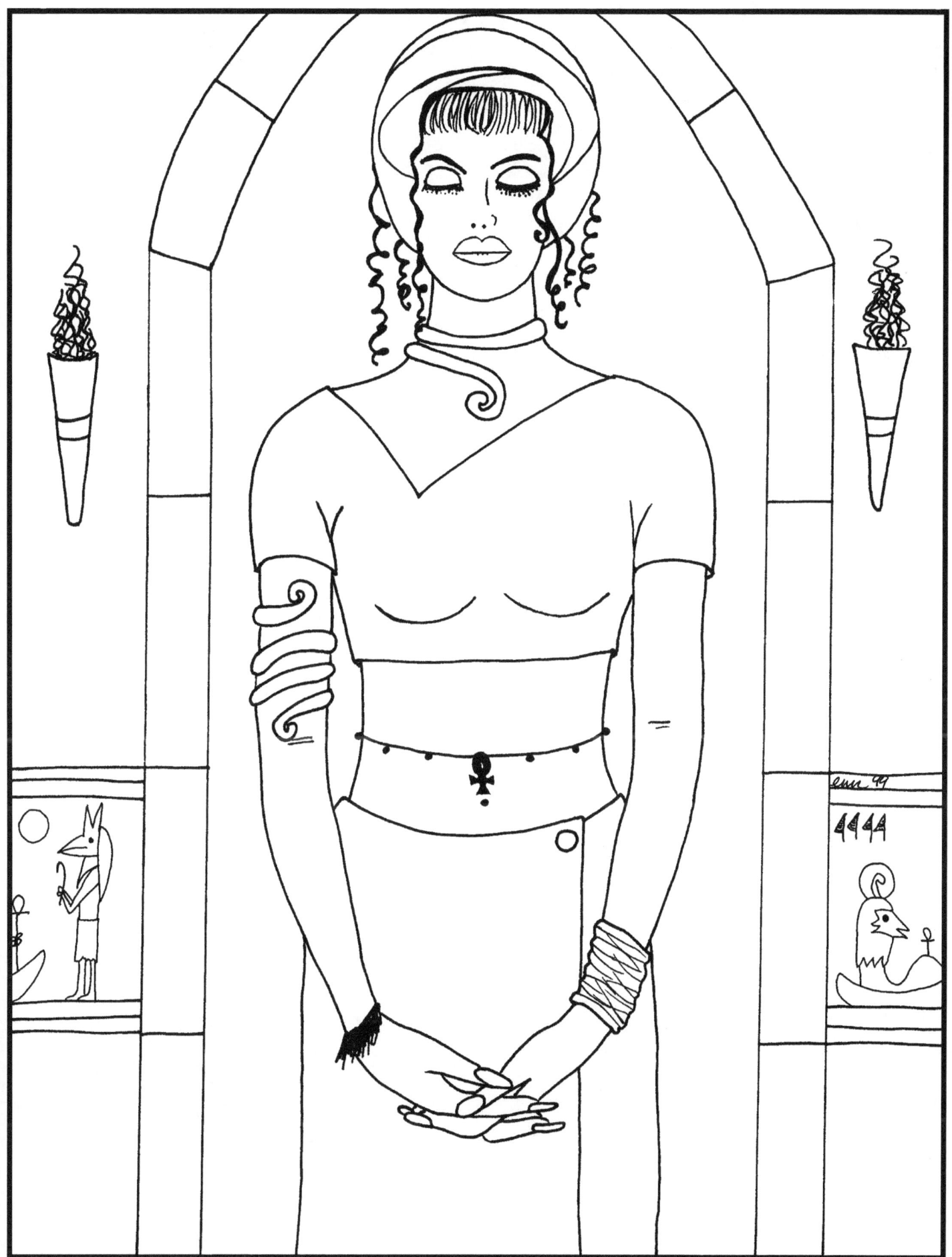

PUNKER SADNESS

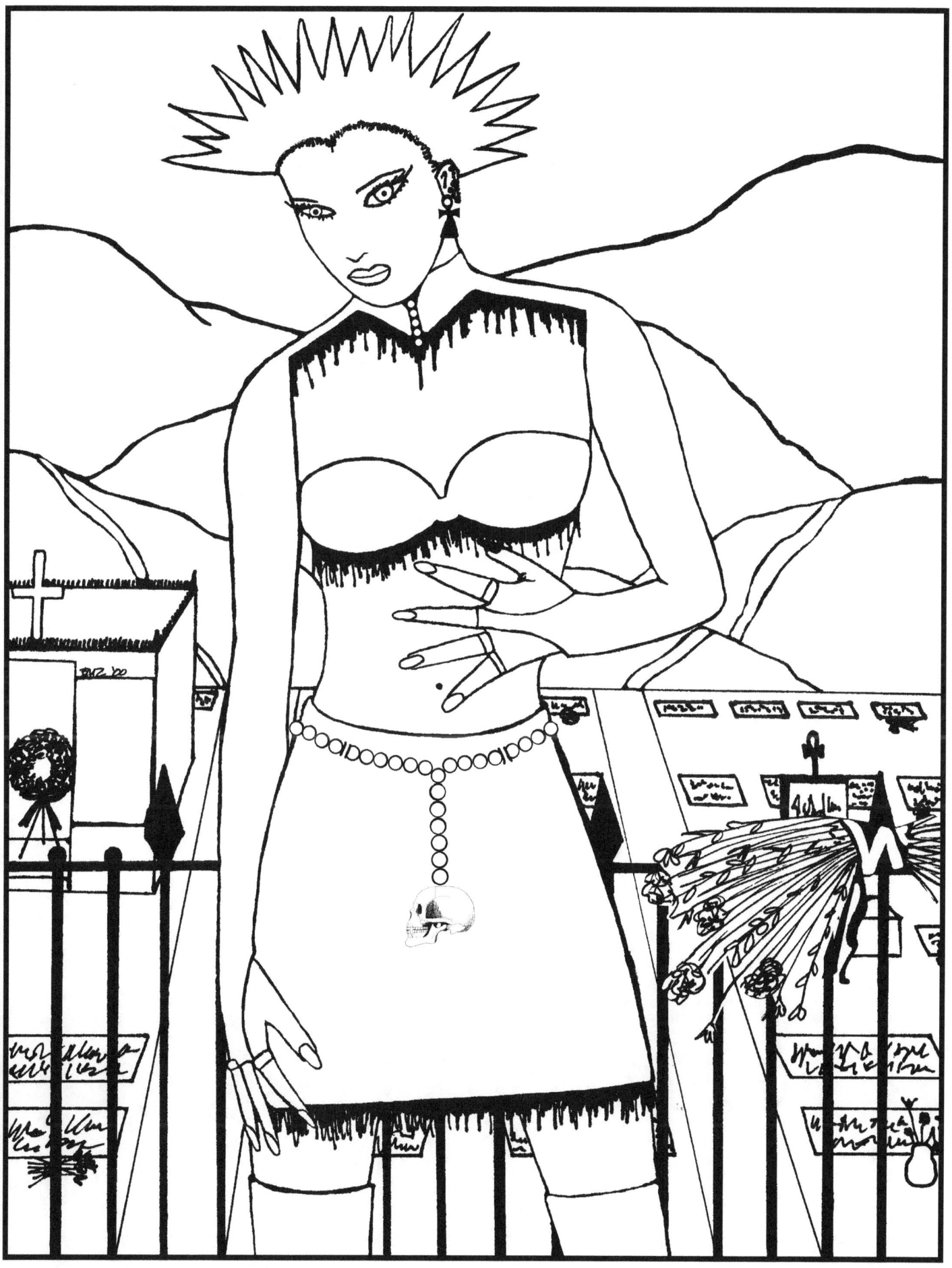

SNAKE CHARMER

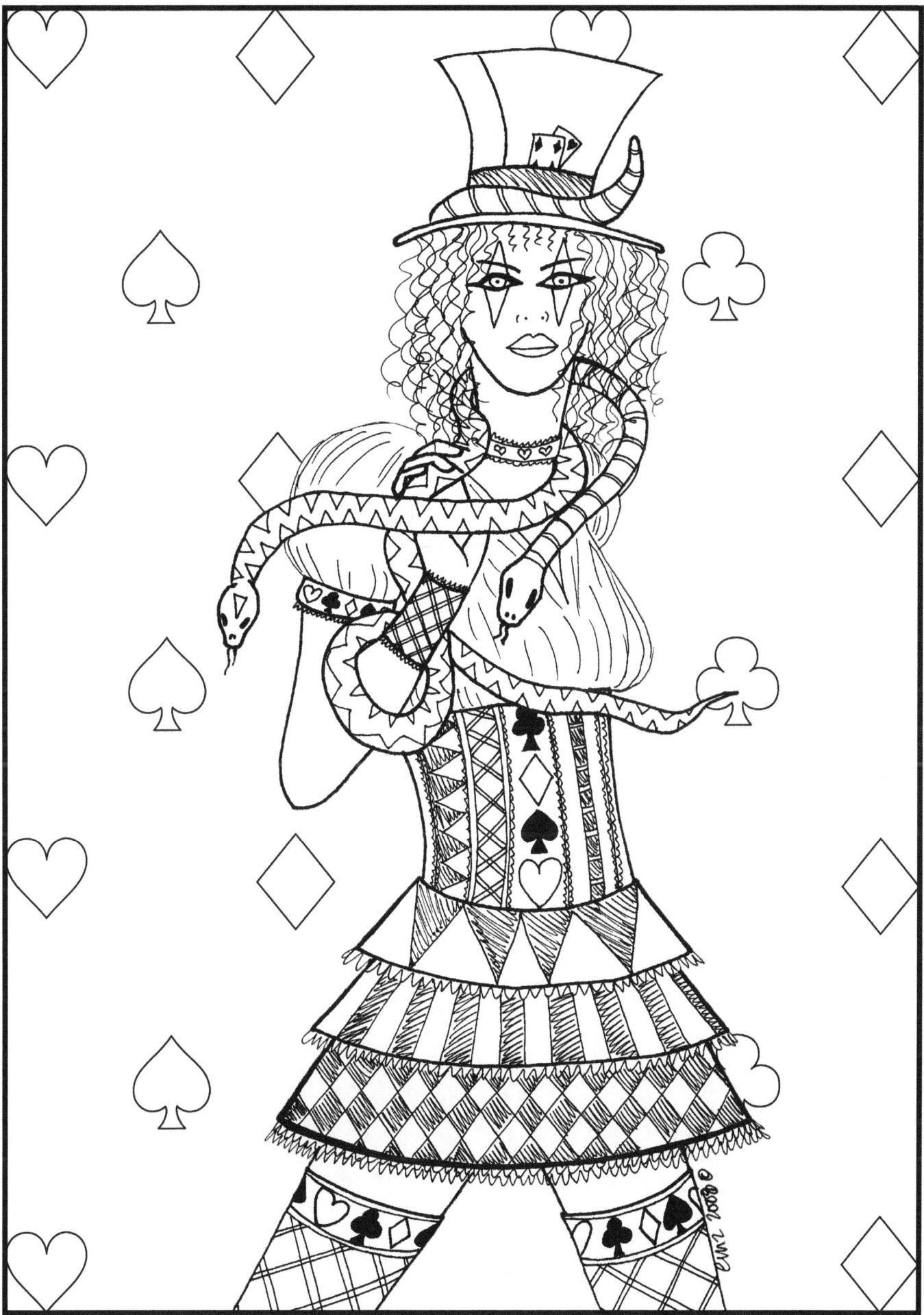

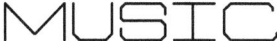

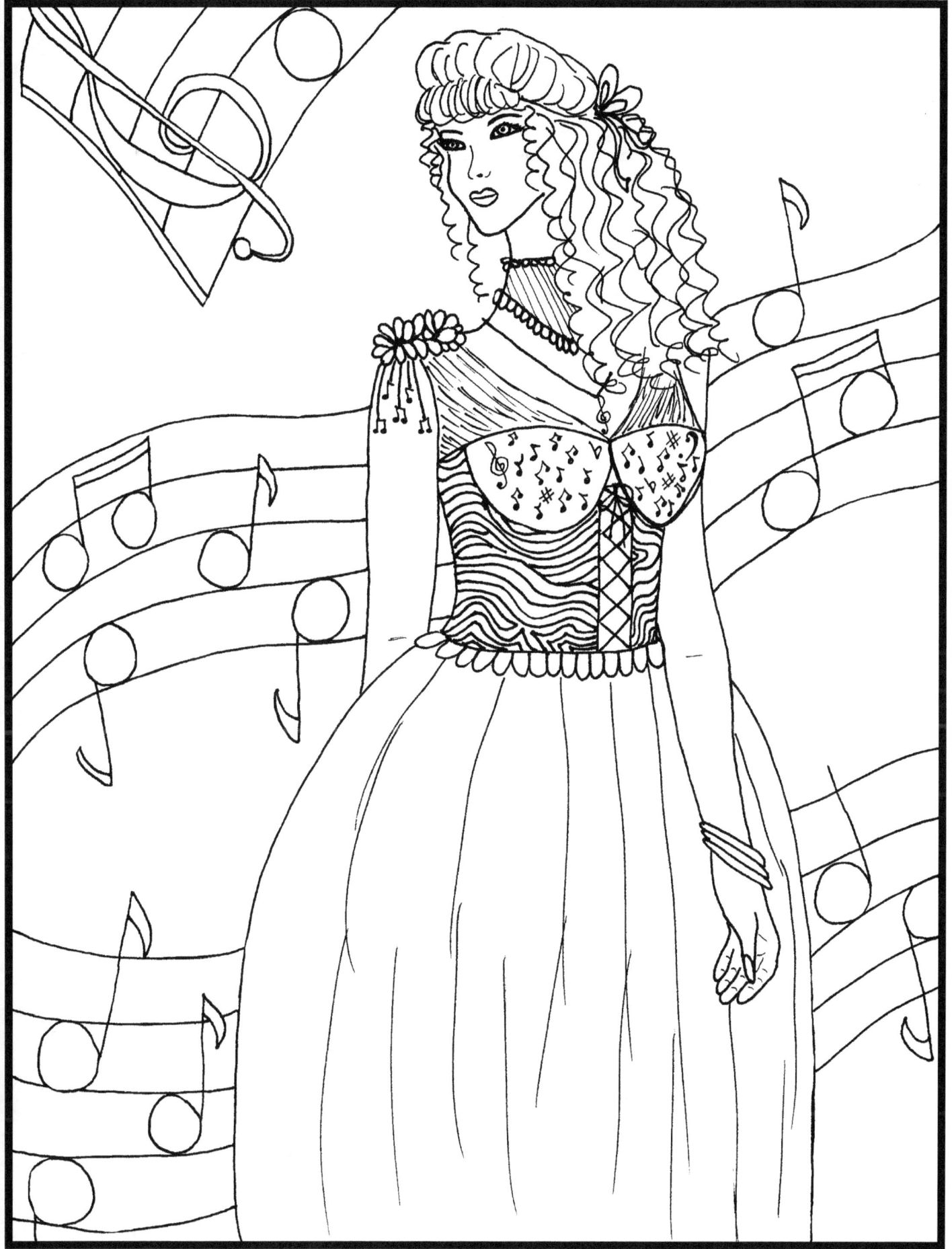

COUTURE LOLI

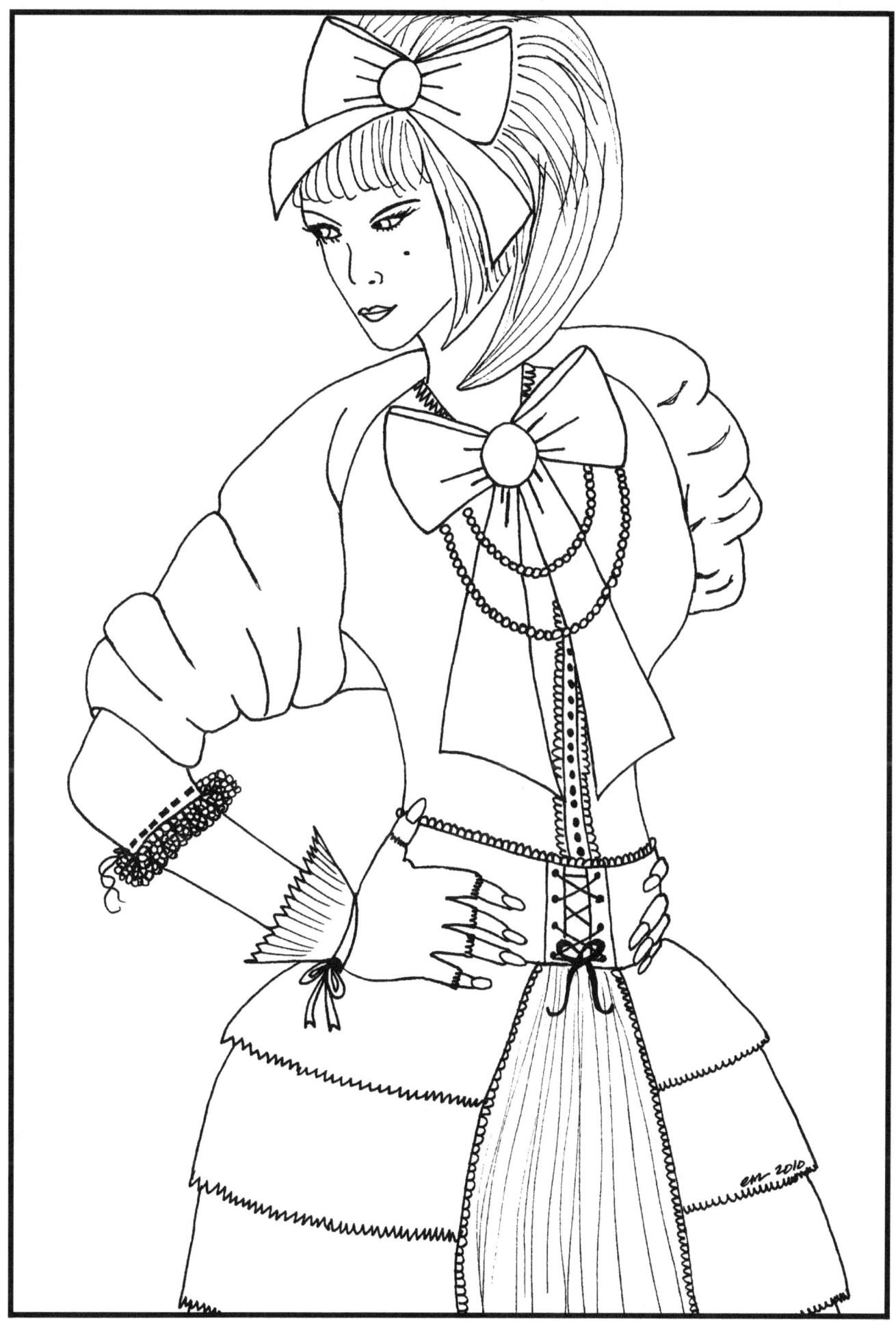

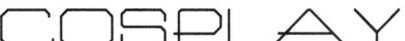

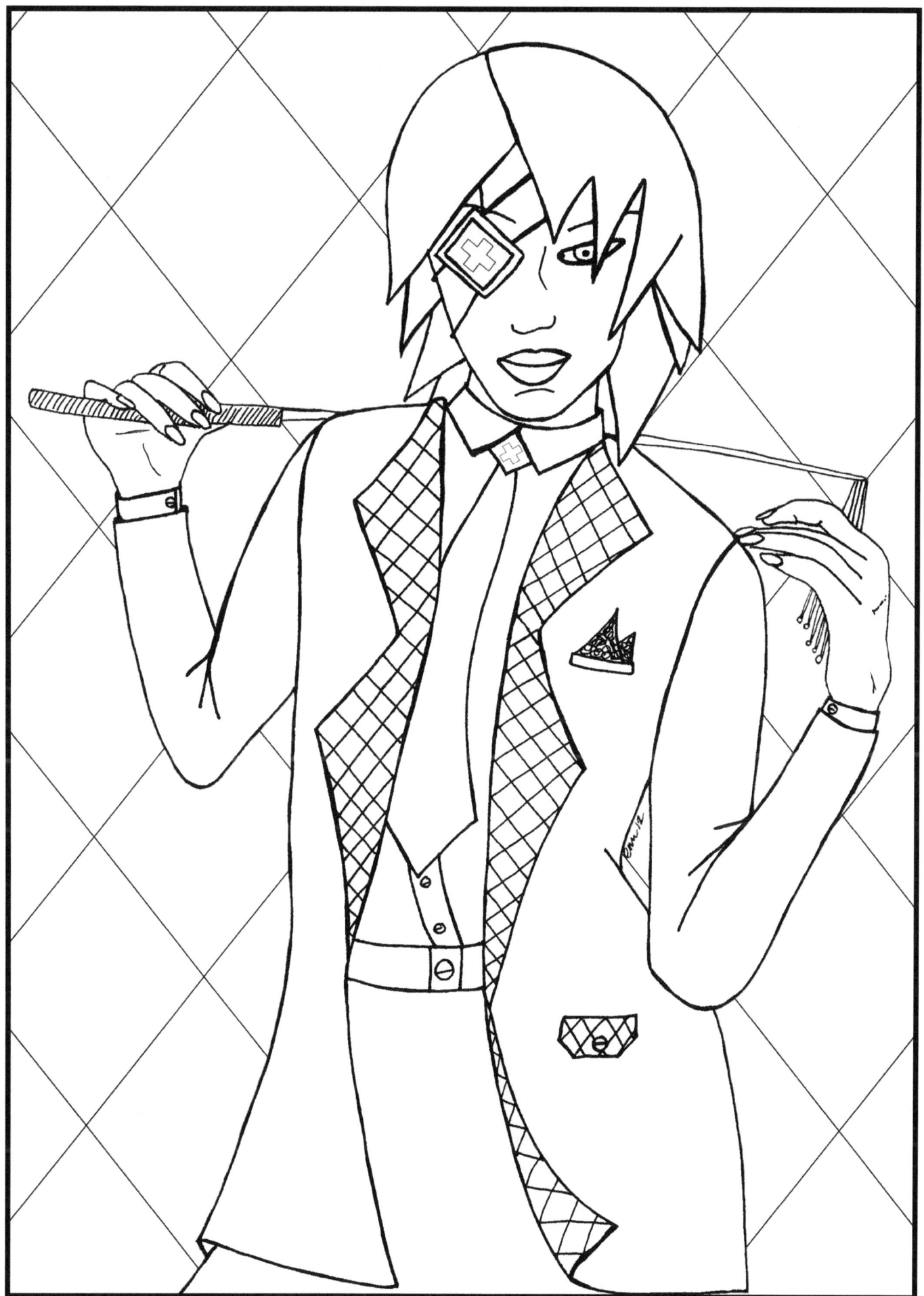

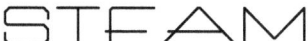

STEAM

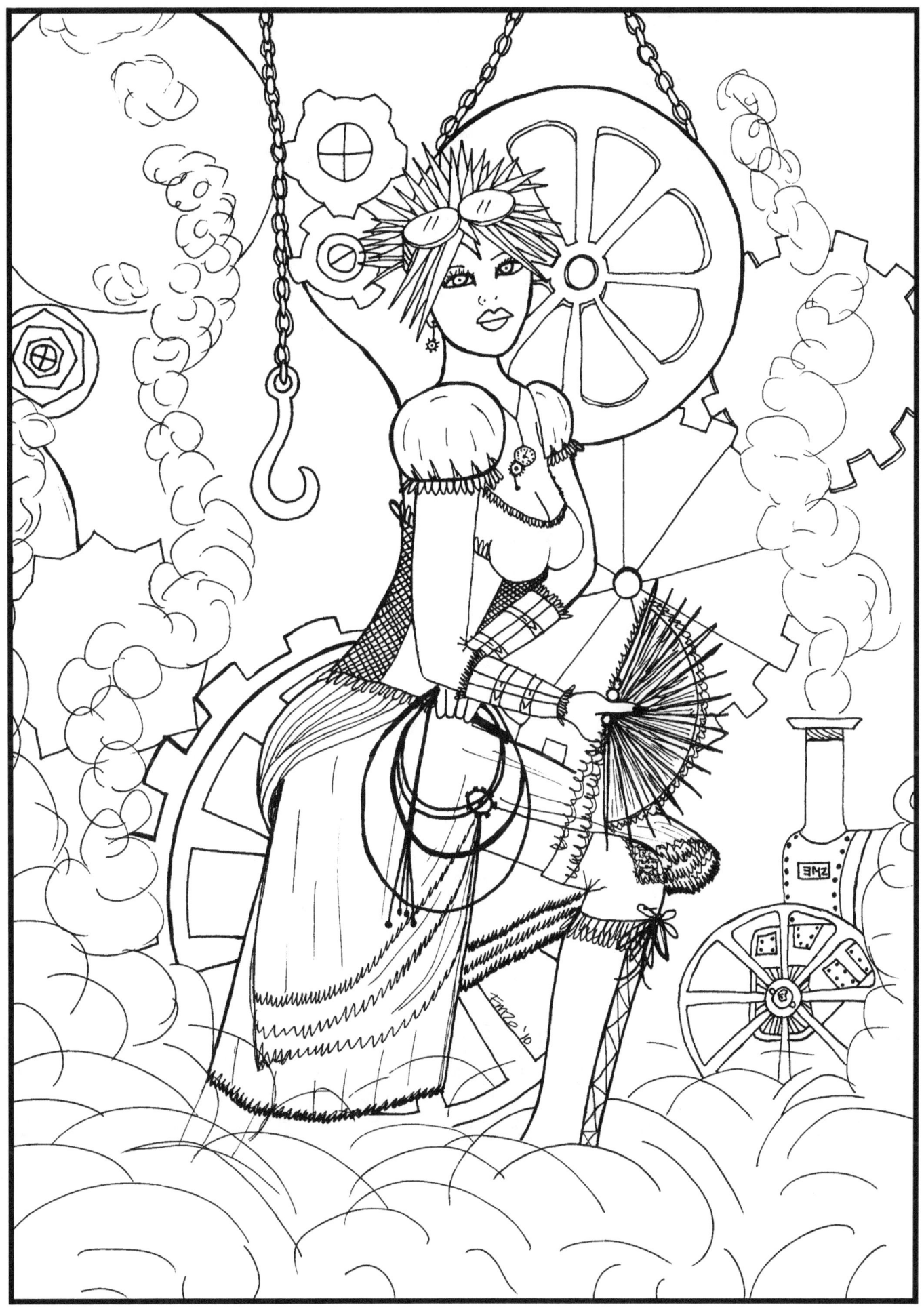

GOTH NUN

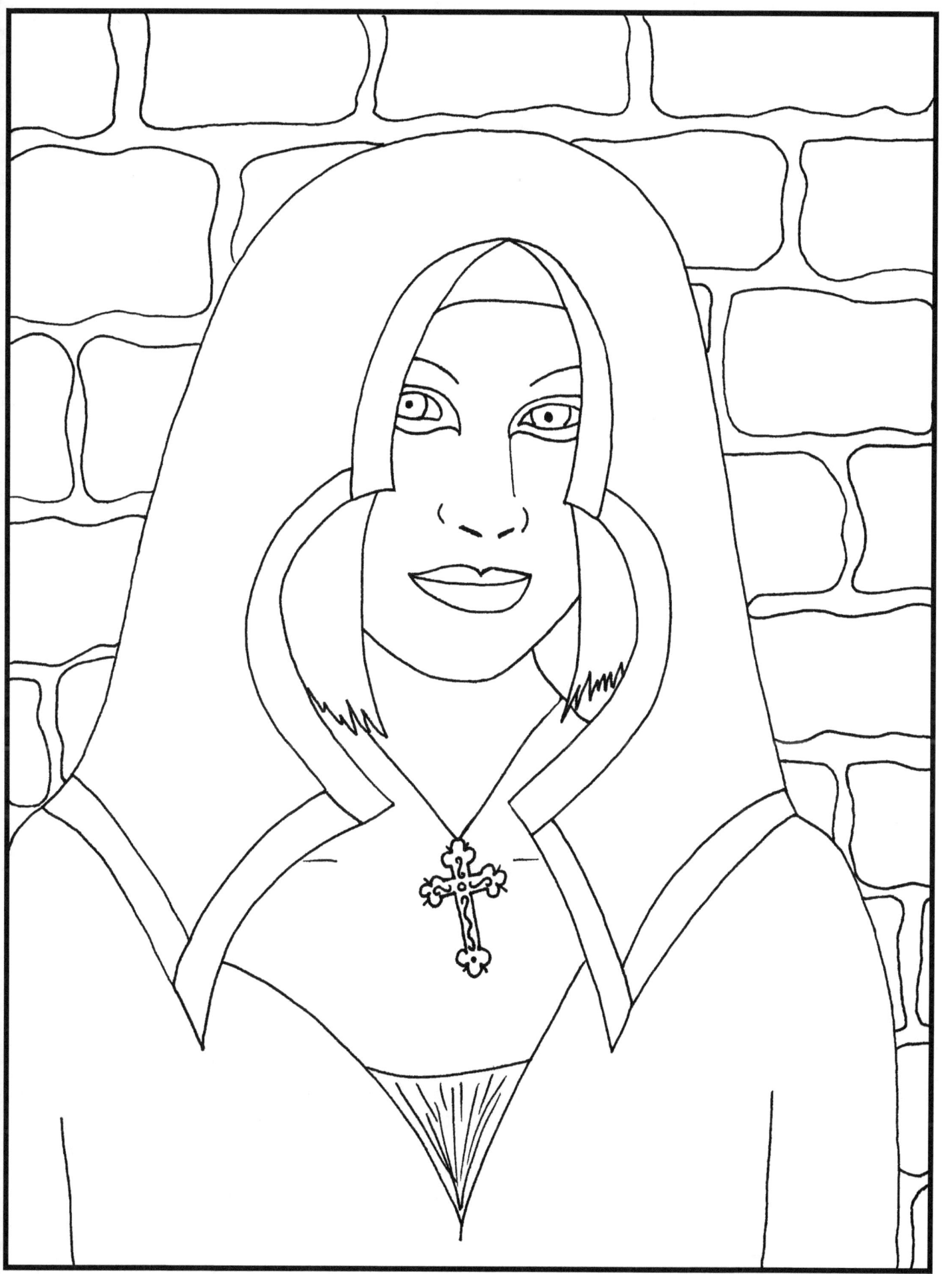

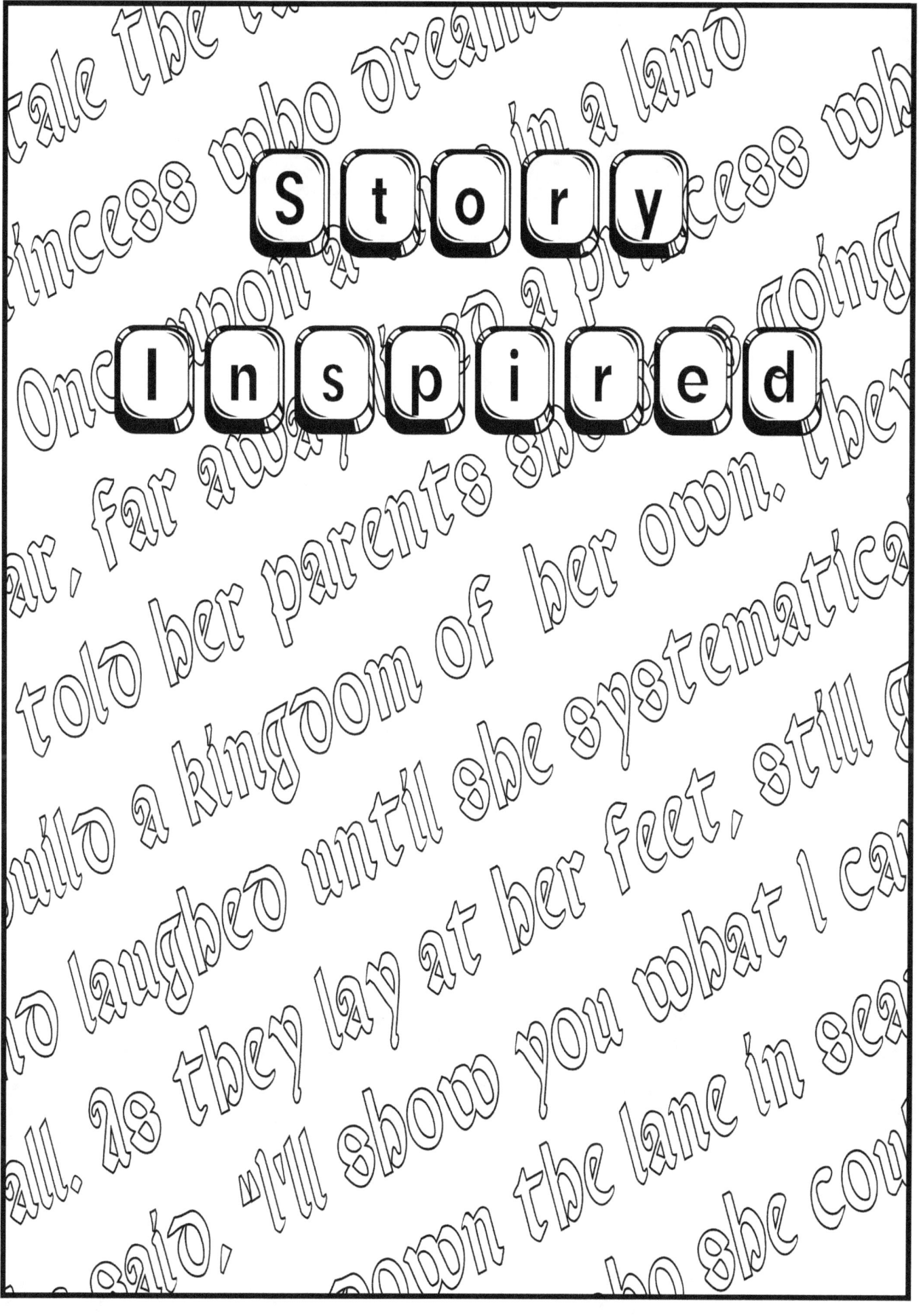

Story Inspired

DEATH OF
THE MACHINES

Based on the story "Death of the Machines" published in *Podthology* by Dragon Moon Press about a man who despises machines, finding he is one of them.

Gripping the flashlight with one hand, he inspected his wound in the mirror. Instead of creamy white bone, something shiny and metallic flickered in the wavering flashlight beam.

His heartbeat increased, his breath coming quick.

"No! I am what they all are. I am a machine!"

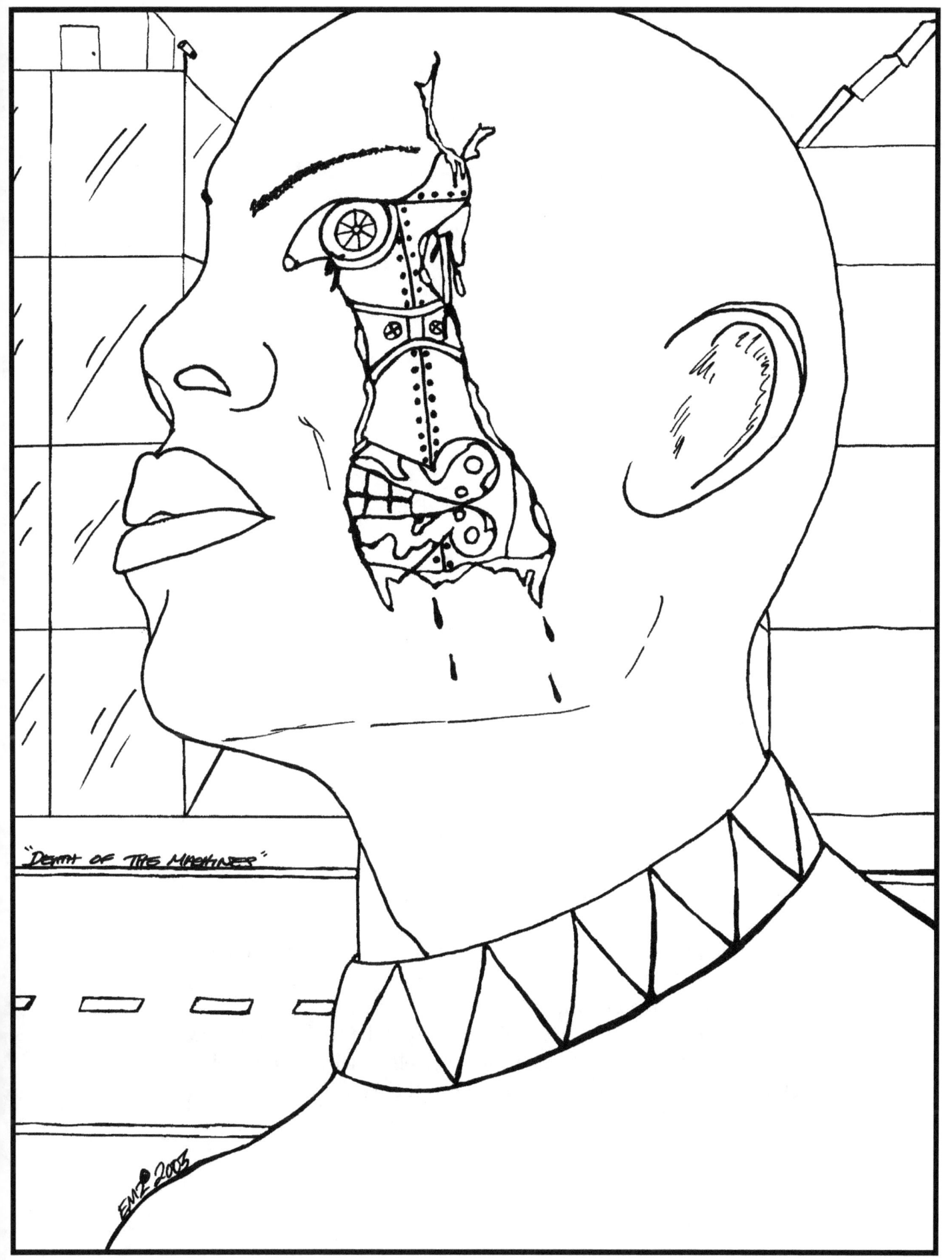

"DEATH OF THE MACHINES"

EMZ 2003

DARK ANGELS

Based on the story "Dark Angels" published in *DarkLives* ezine about a young girl who witnesses a battle between angels.

"Get her," he growled. Throwing off his coat, he exposed massive black wings.

Ten pairs of wings surrounded me in minutes. I was never going to get out of their dark clutches.

A high-pitched voice came out of the darkness, making the dark ones clutch their ears and recoil into black feathered balls. Up over their hunched bodies came a bright light.

"Kiley, you are not safe here," the being said, sweeping me up with her white wings and carrying me to safety, away from the dark monsters.

Her wings were as soft as my bed at home and held me tight as we soared through the air to a branch out over the dark things who woke from their delirium.

"Hold on to the tree. Don't let go. We'll be back." In the trees around me where tons of angels like herself. Their white hair blew behind them as they swooped down onto the dark beings.

Screams filled the air as the fight of the angels began.

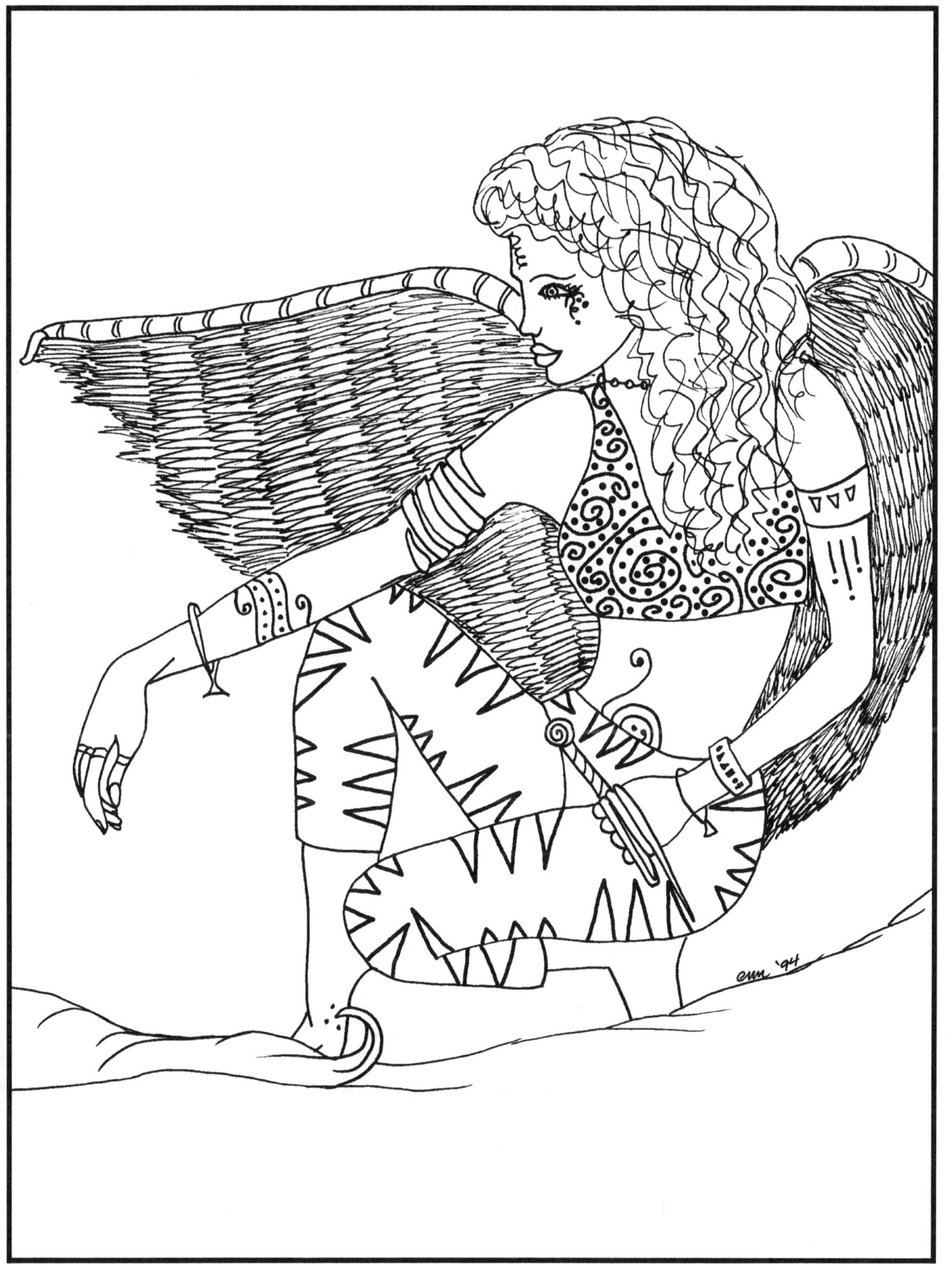

DARK SOUL

Based on the poem "Dark Soul"

By: Emerian Rich
If the world was as dark as my soul...
But it isn't, I'm isolated

What a powdered, pink mother
Gives birth to is all her
Fear of death.

But we aren't scared anymore, are we?

A childhood of fear has turned into
Hopelessness,
Helplessness,
Finally, fearlessness.

We are strong aren't we?
We are jaded and mean.
We are heartless and rude.

Sometimes I cry at the things I've done,
For loving myself,
For doing what I want.

Where do I go to get rid of the guilt
From that house with the white picket fence?

I try to drown it in all types of poison.
Torture to my body and soul.

But there's no hope at last
I'm dying from it.
The guilt of my mother's past.

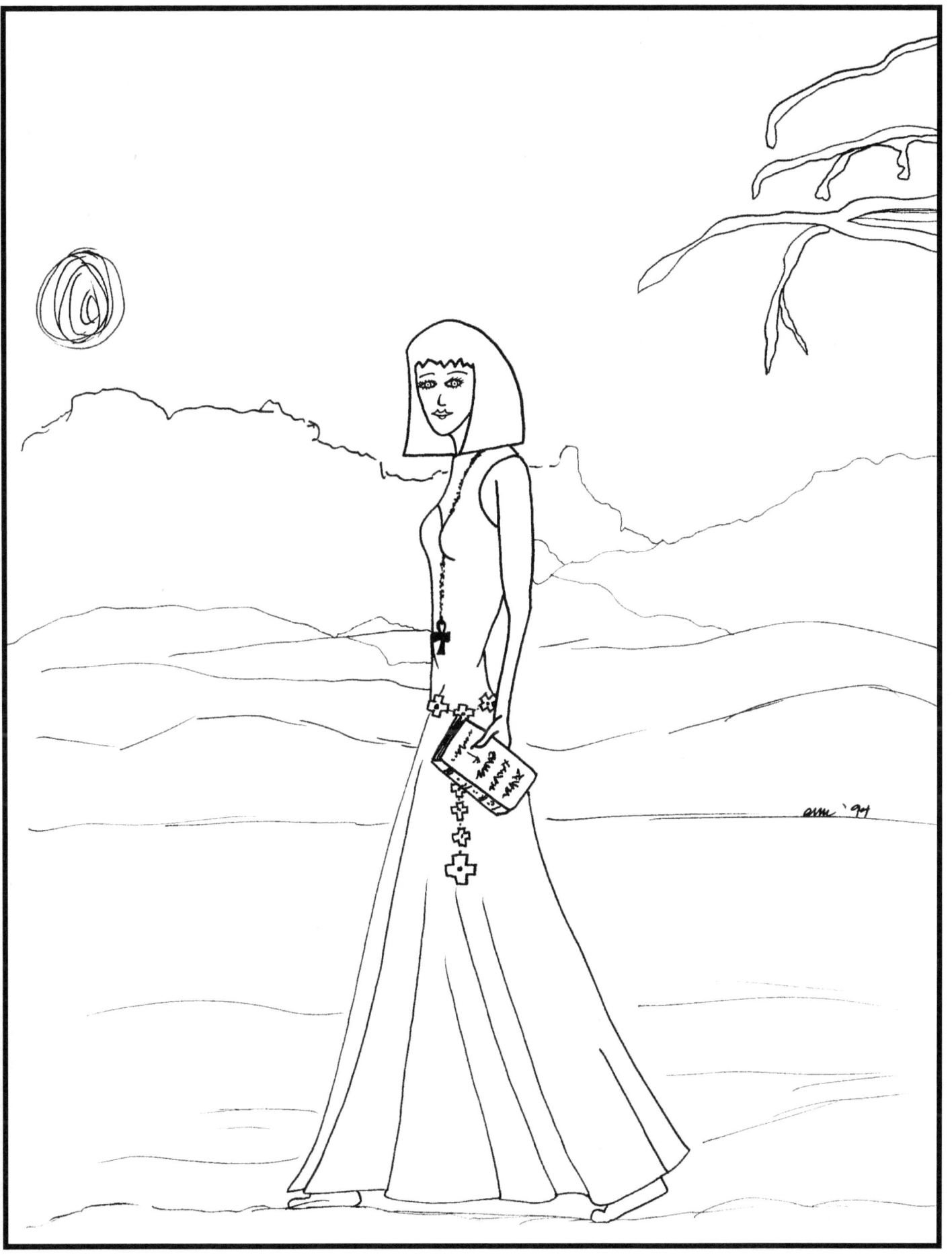

SEVERINA

Based on the character Severina Santos from the vampire novel *Night's Knights*.

Severina is an exotic beauty from the jungles of Brazil whose family is brutally murdered by the same man she later calls lover. Born in 1485 and brought over as a vampire in 1502, Severina is a young woman when brought into the life, but becomes the mother figure in *Night's Knights*.

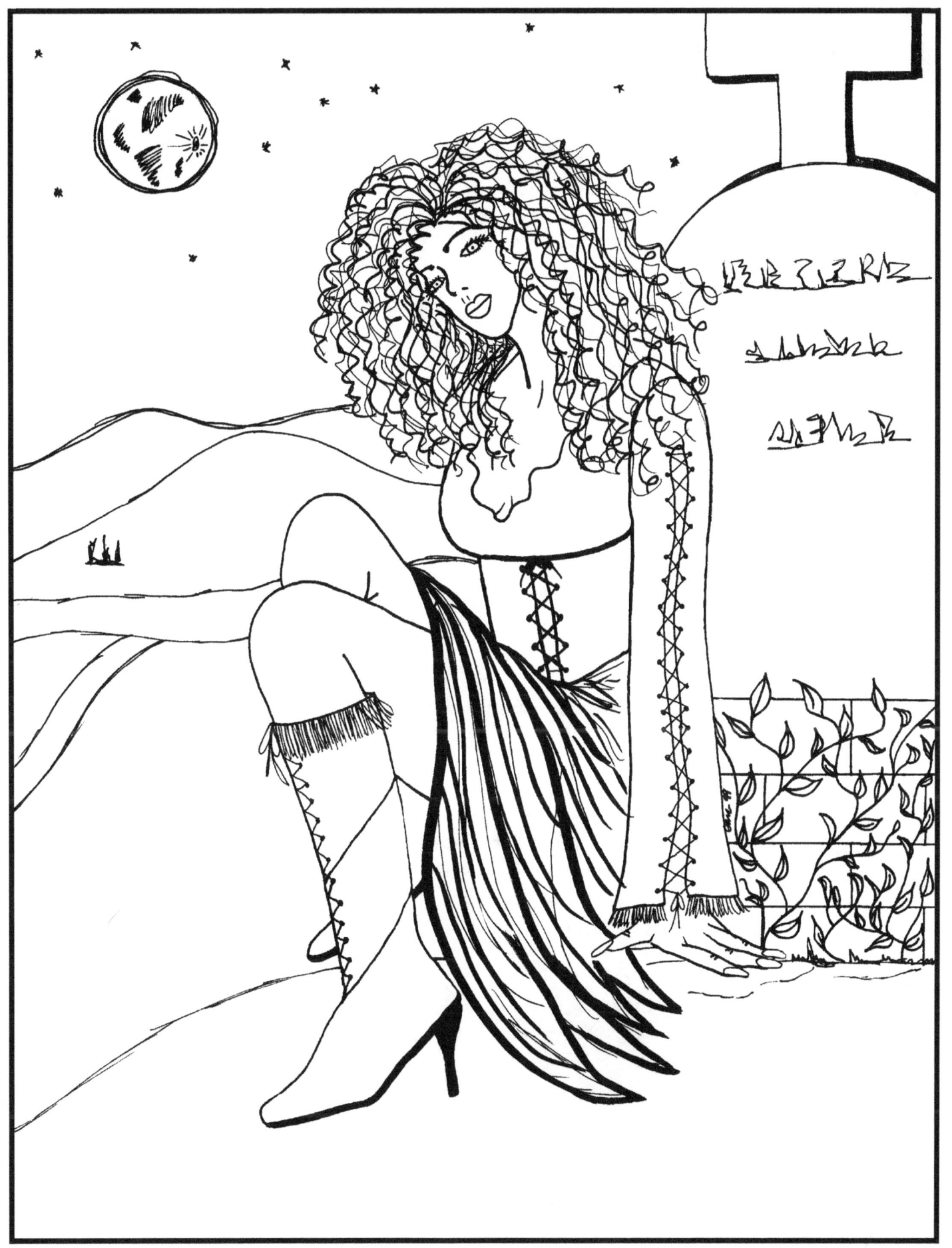

KRISTINE

Based on the character Kristine from the vampire novel *Night's Knights*.

One of the Chosen Ones, Kristine is a mortal girl with a hard life who Julien turned into a vampire out of compassion. He hoped to give her a better life, but her journey is not the one he envisioned for her. She does not thrive in vampire life, but does manage to help bring about the destruction of their enemy.

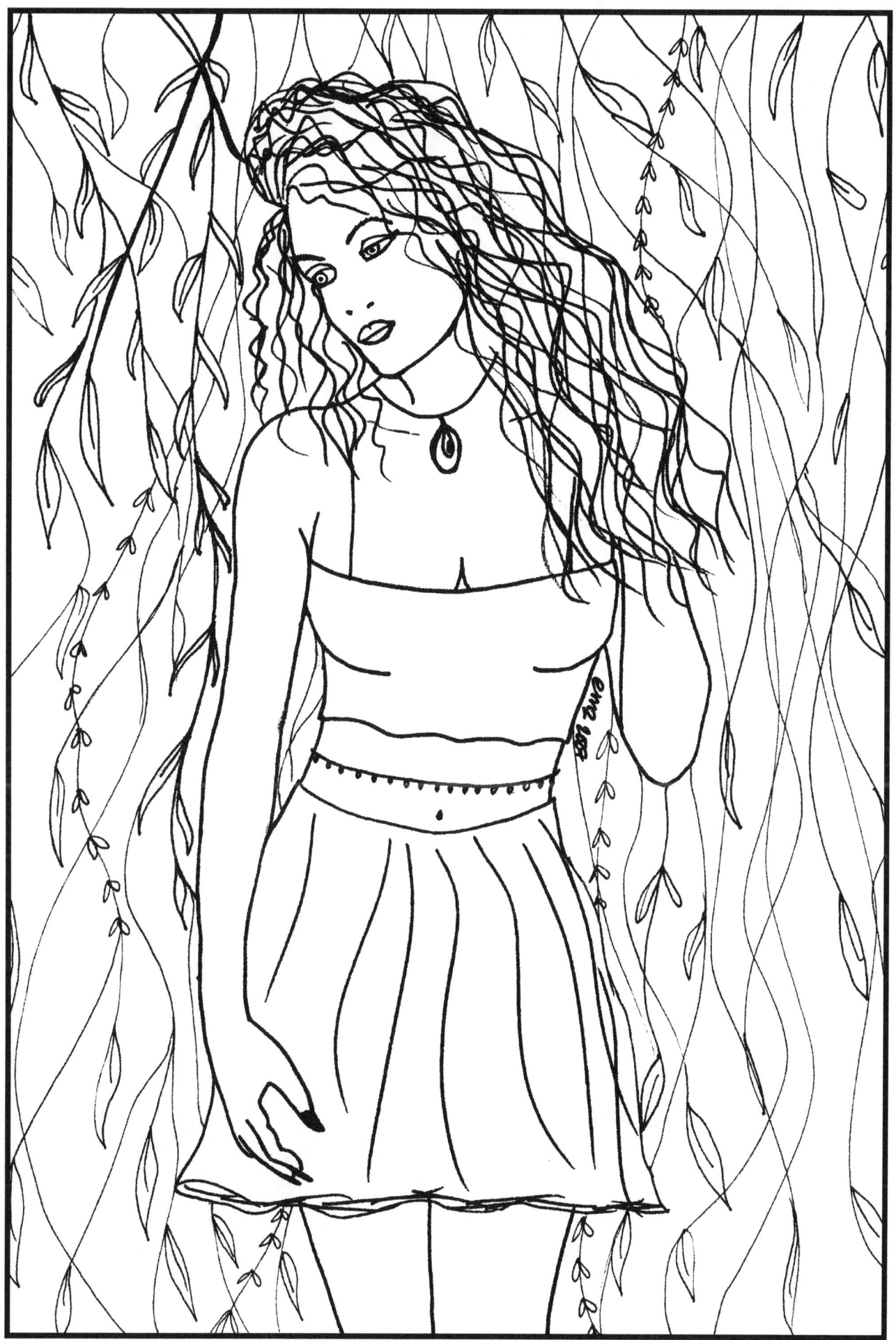

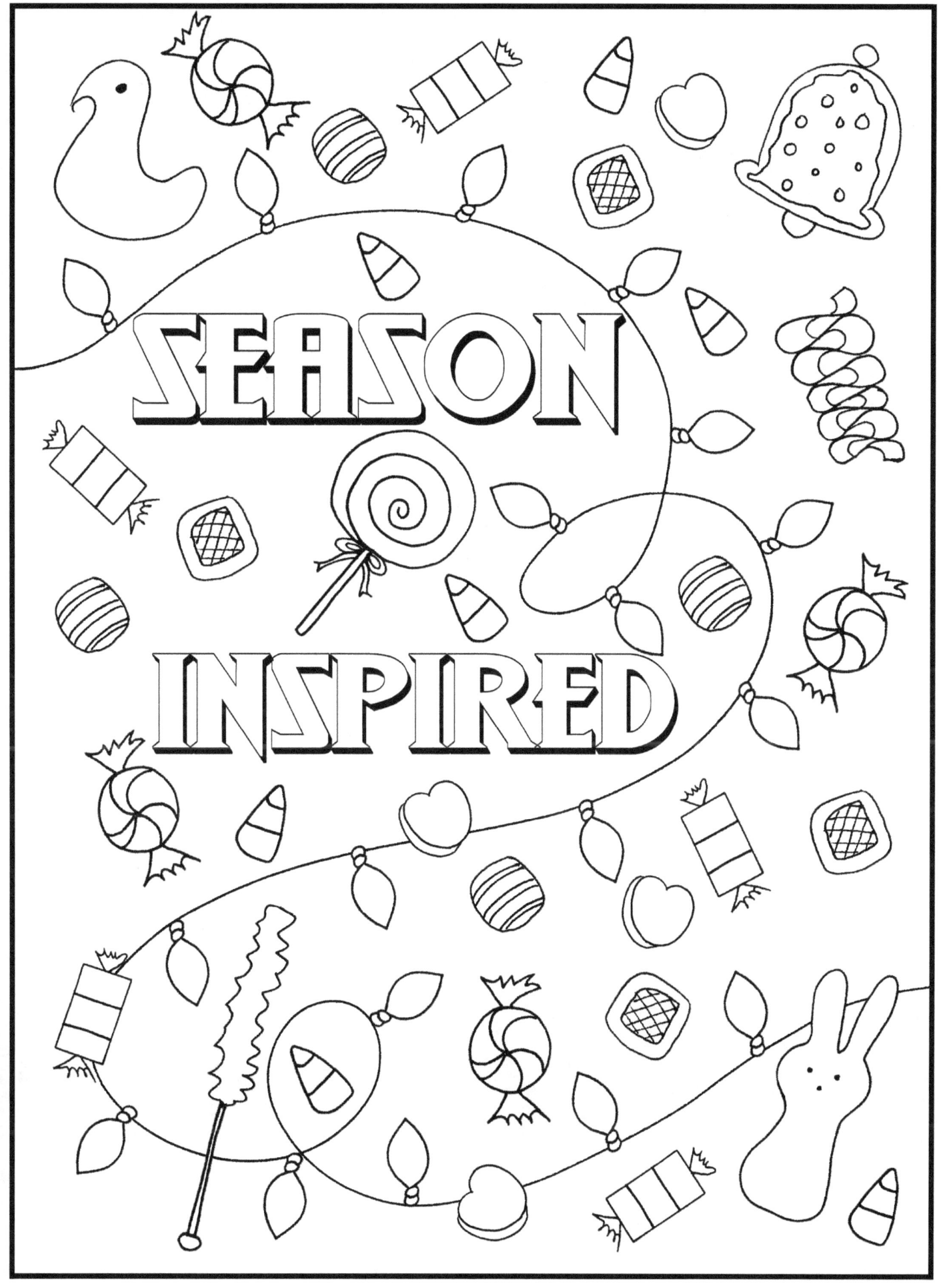

SPRING

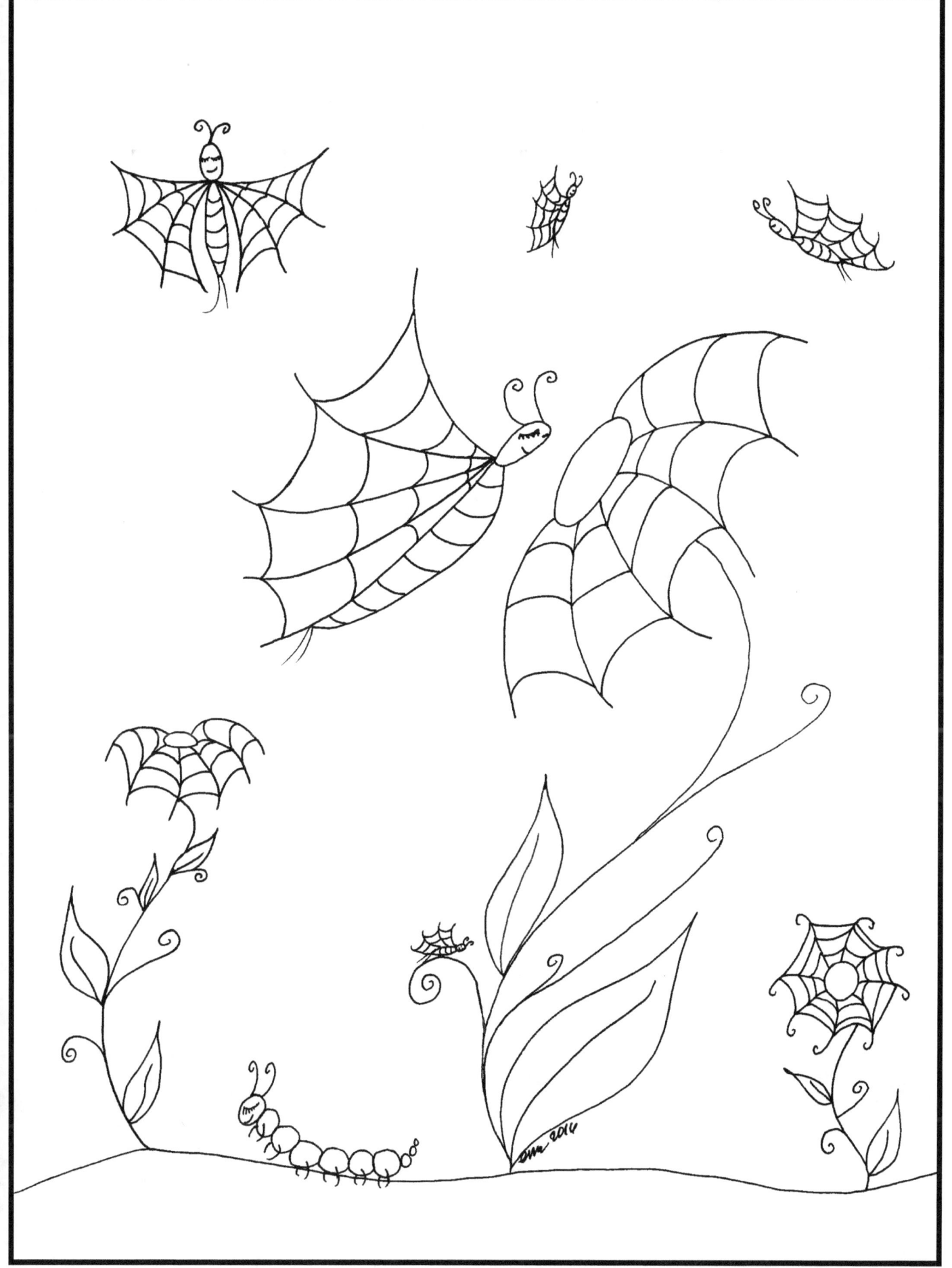

SUMMER

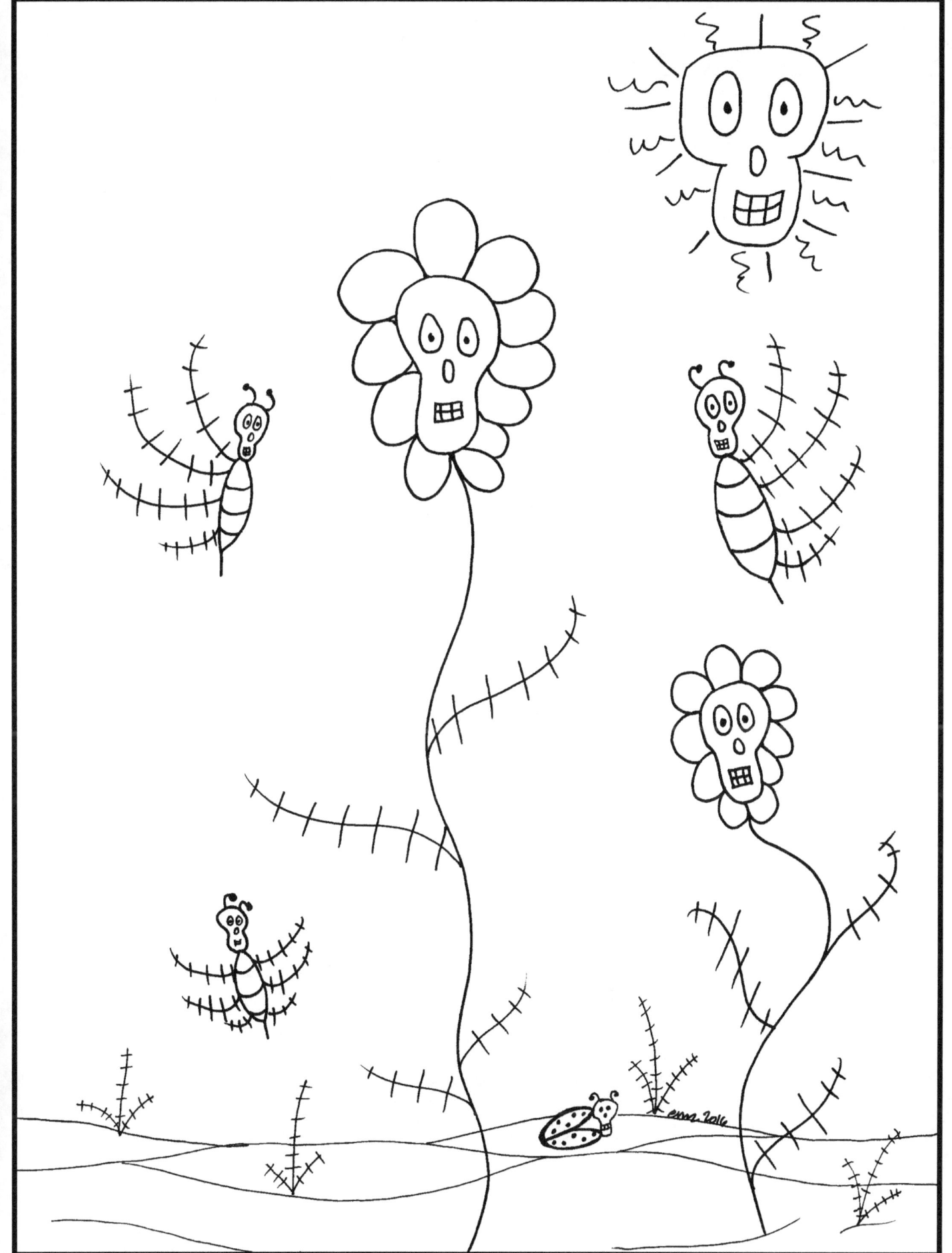

FALL

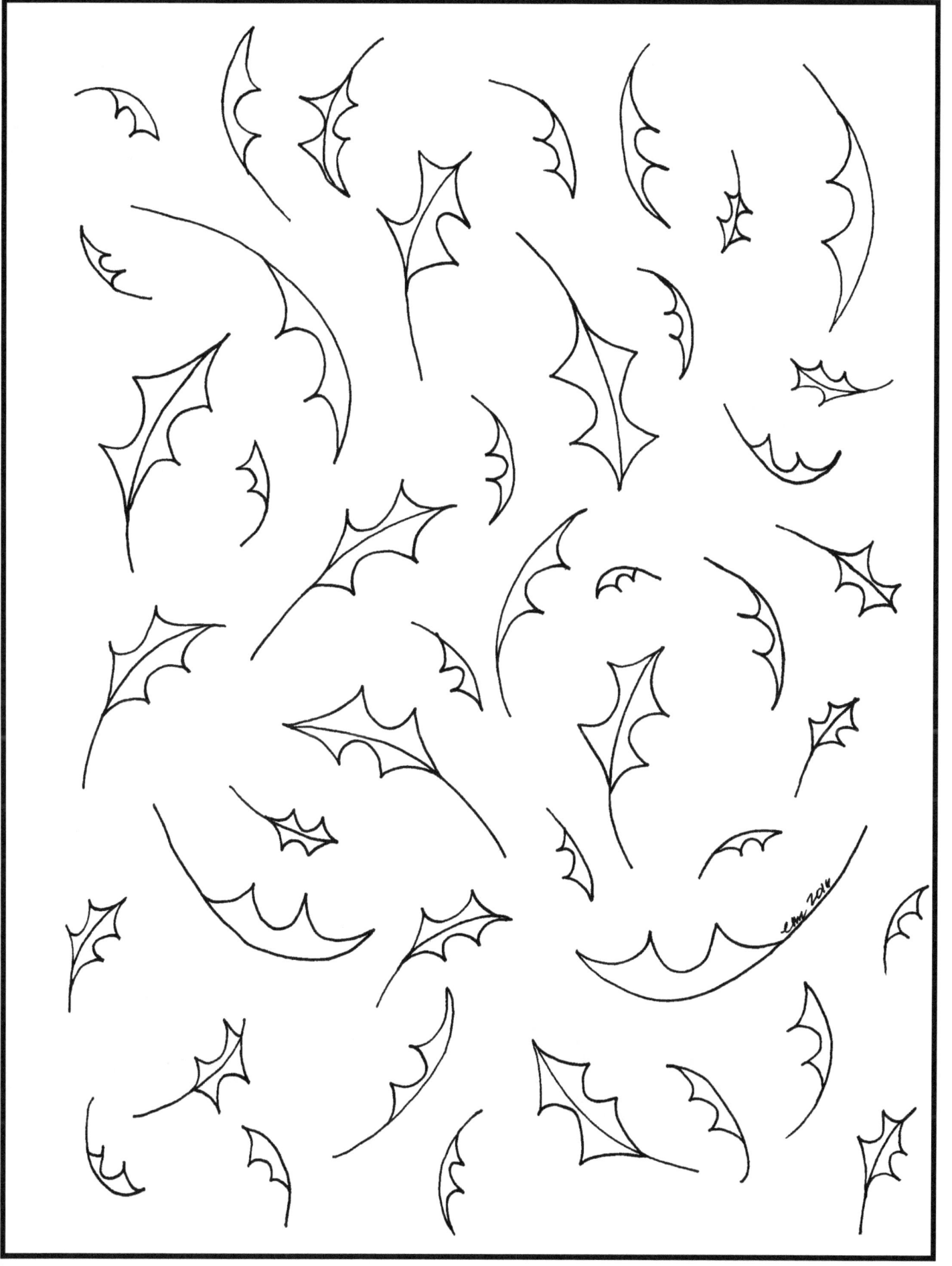

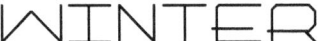
WINTER

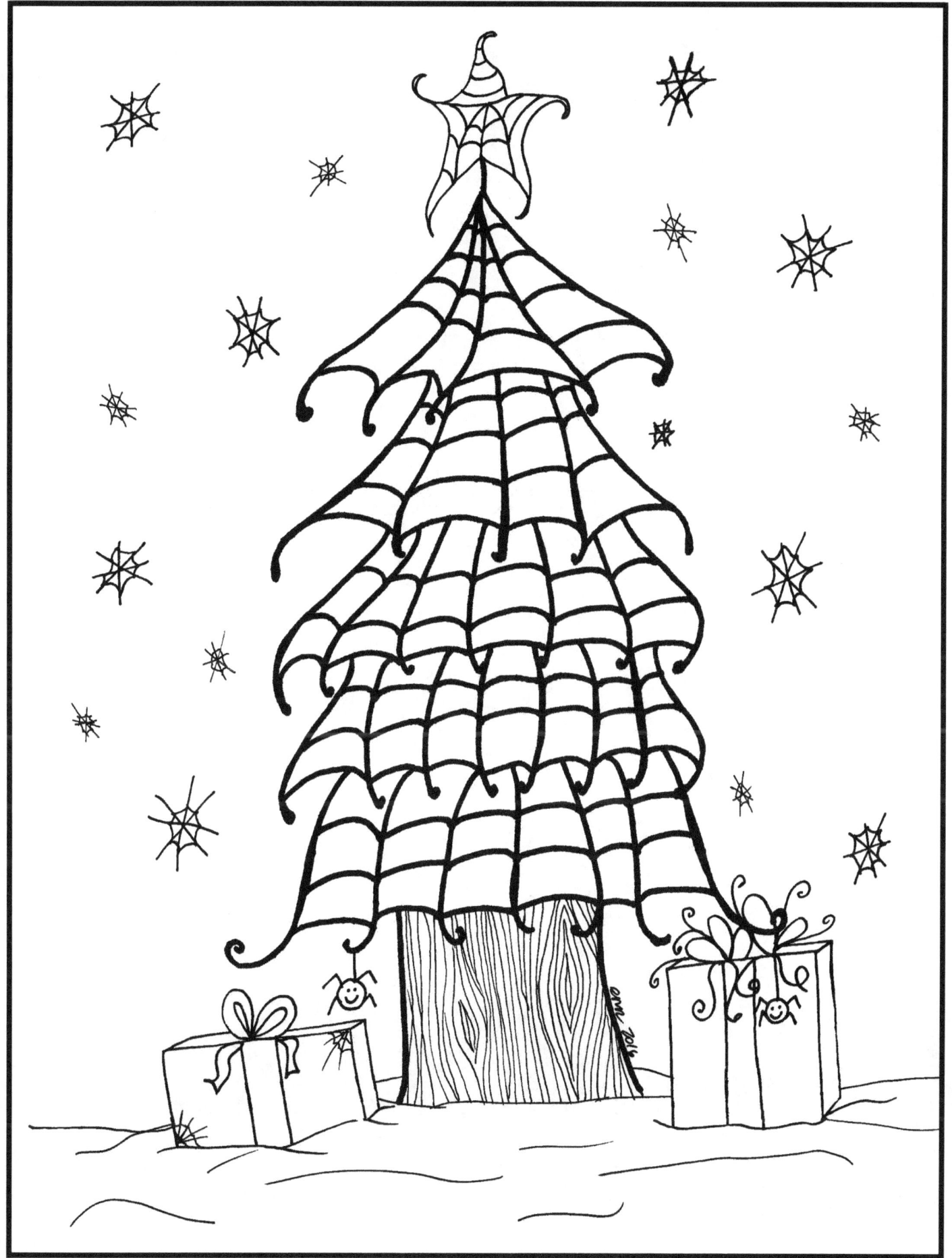

BATTY VALENTINE

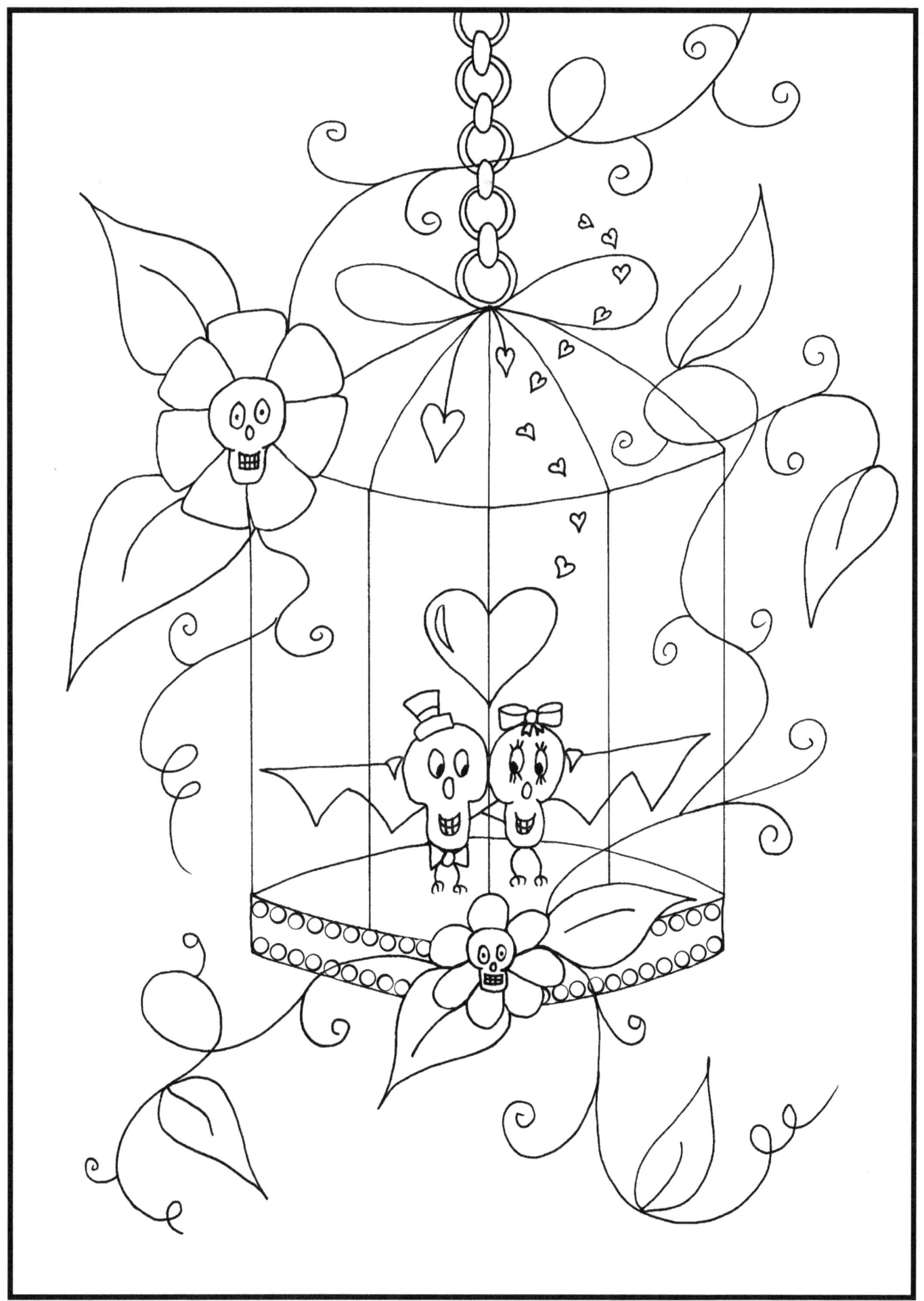

SEA LIFE

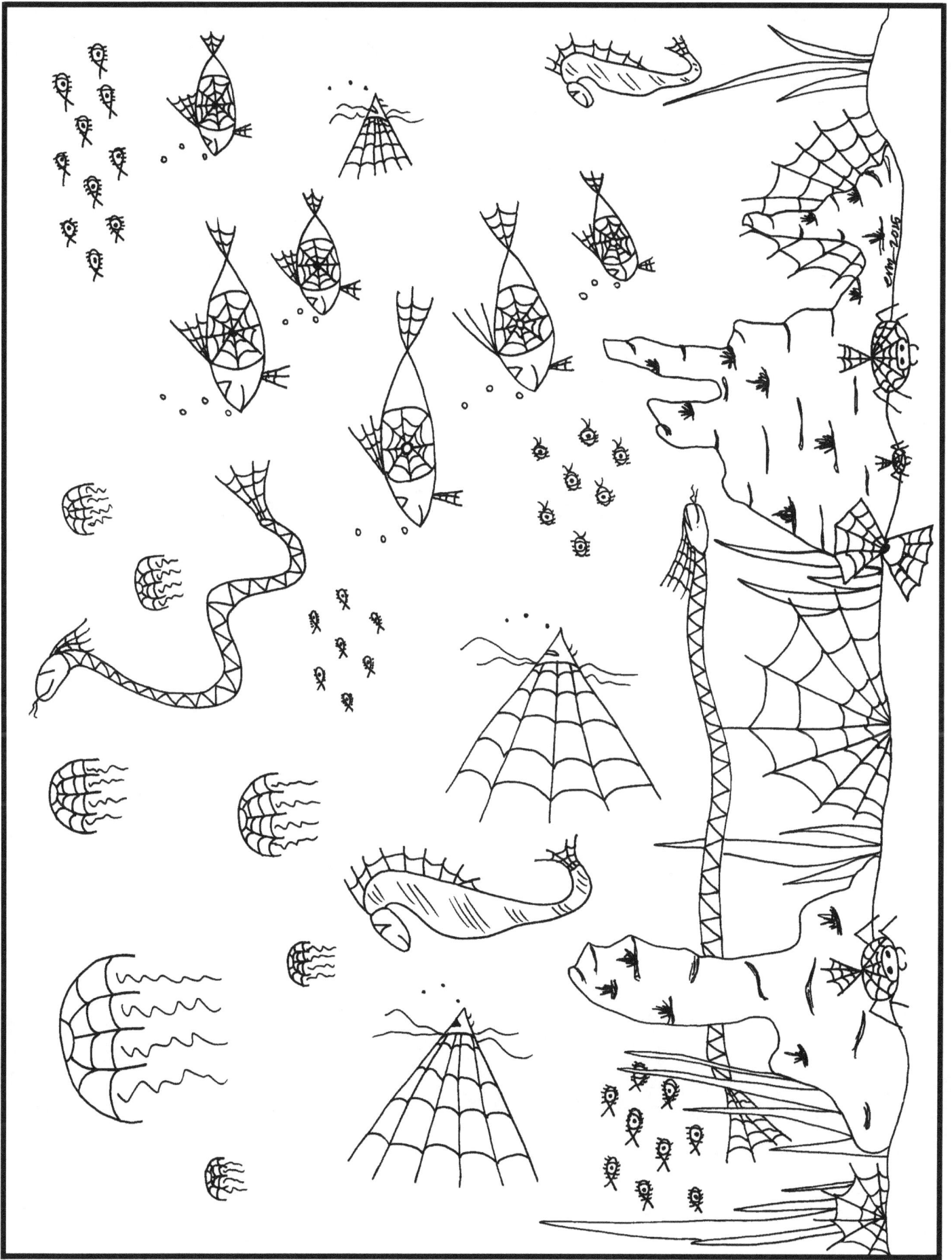

FALL TEA TIME

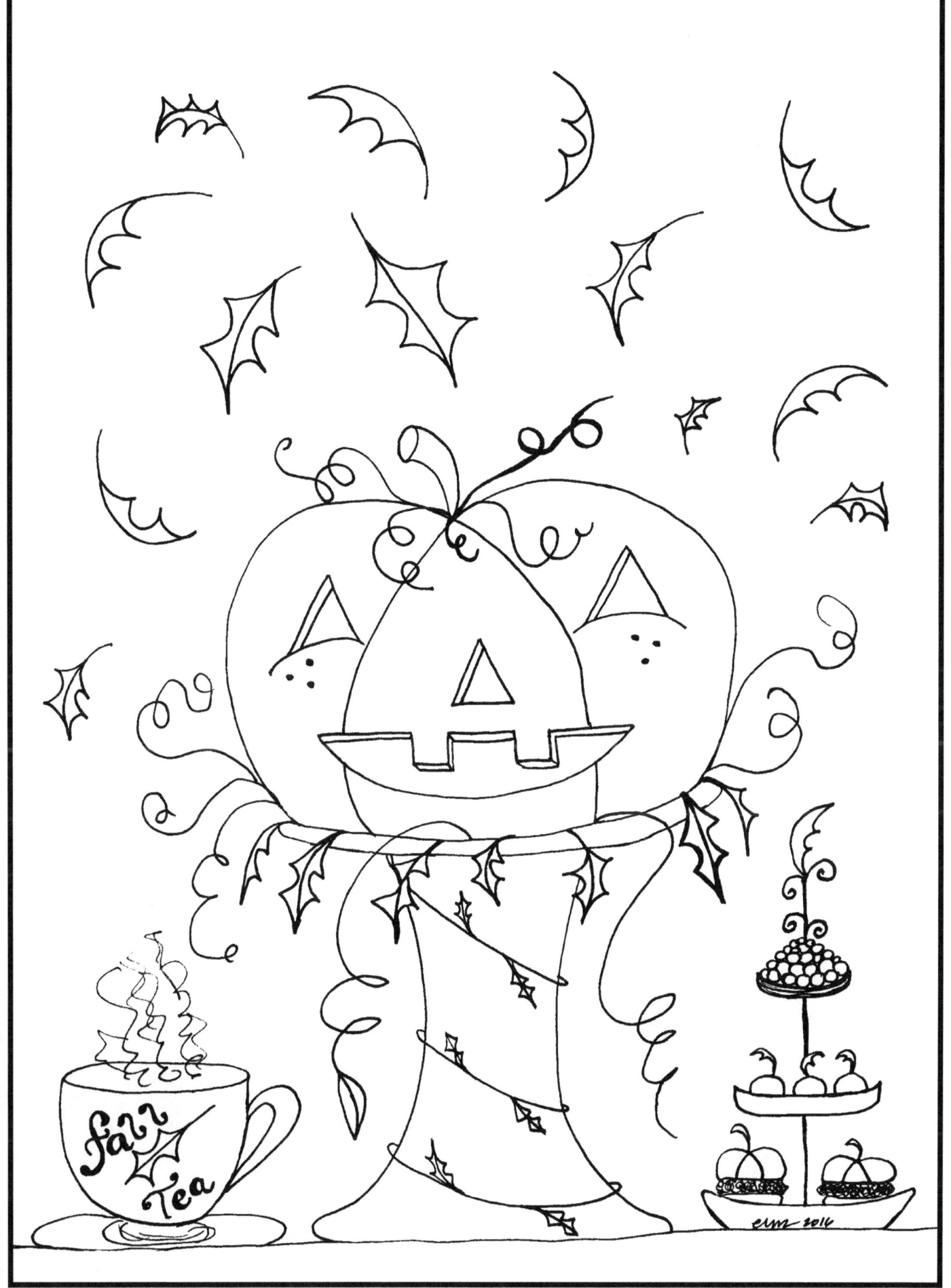

HALLOWEEN

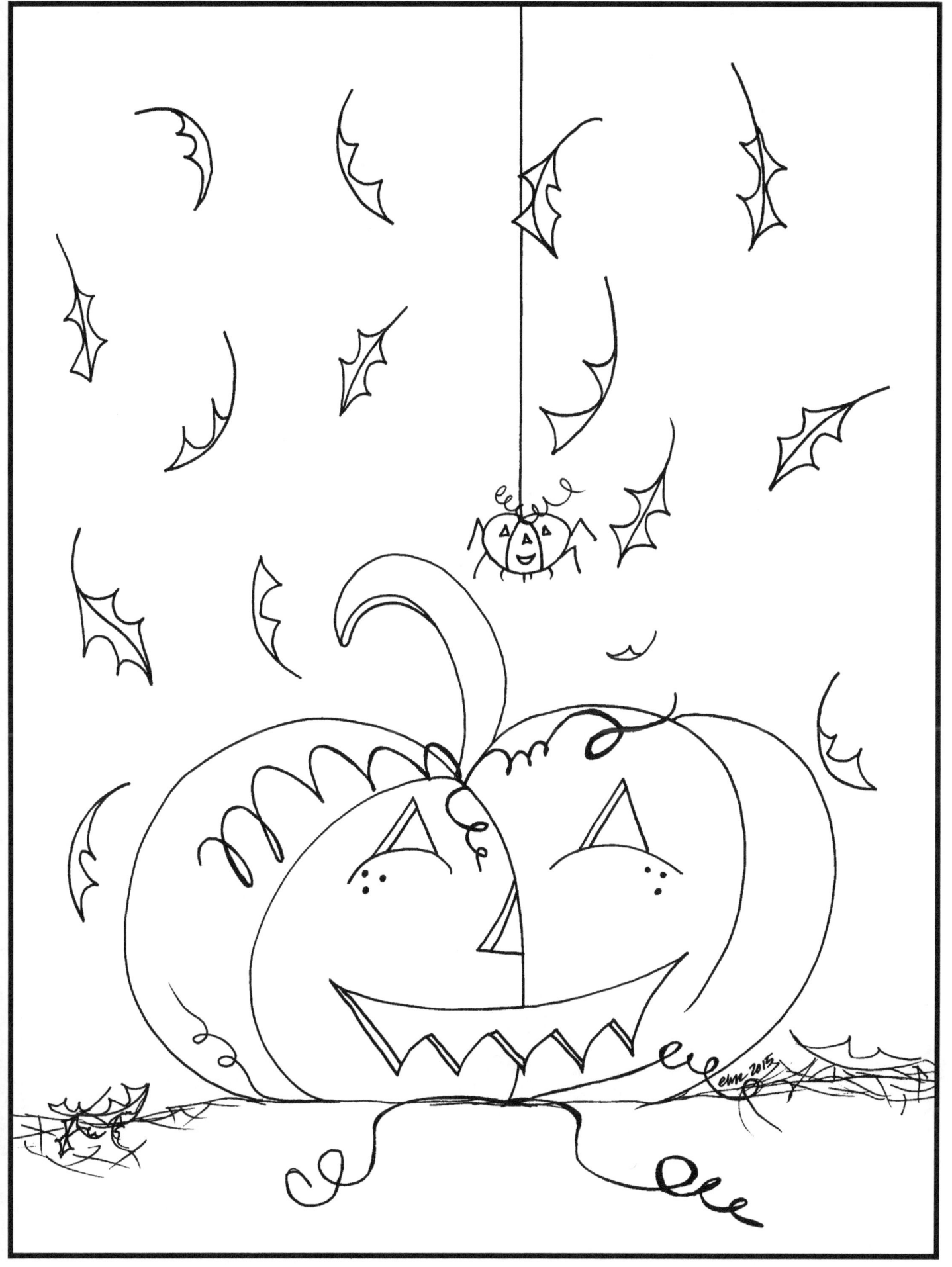

PUMPKIN PATCHIN'

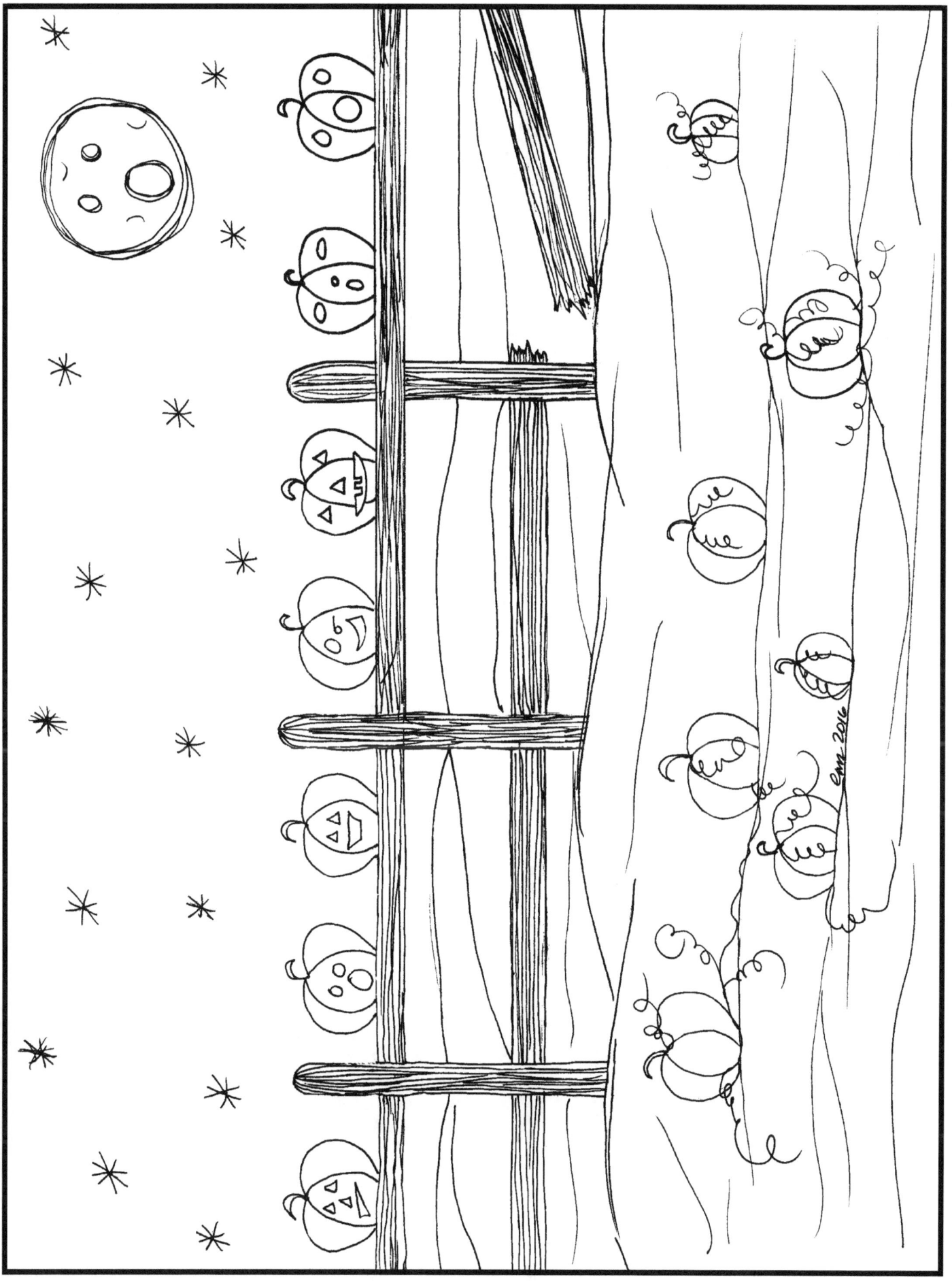

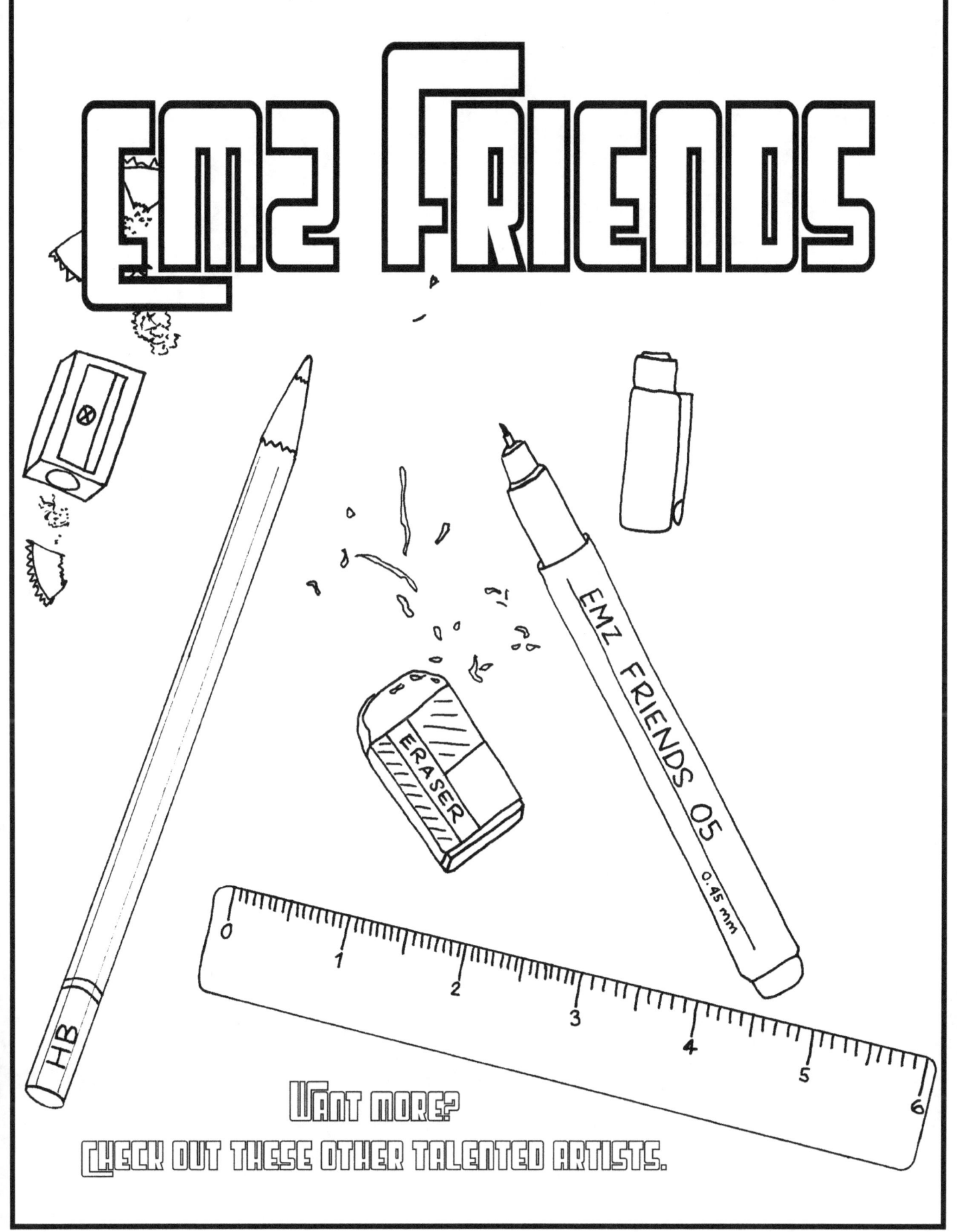

EMZ FRIENDS

EMZ FRIENDS 05
0.45 mm

ERASER

HB

Want more?
Check out these other talented artists.

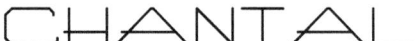
CHANTAL

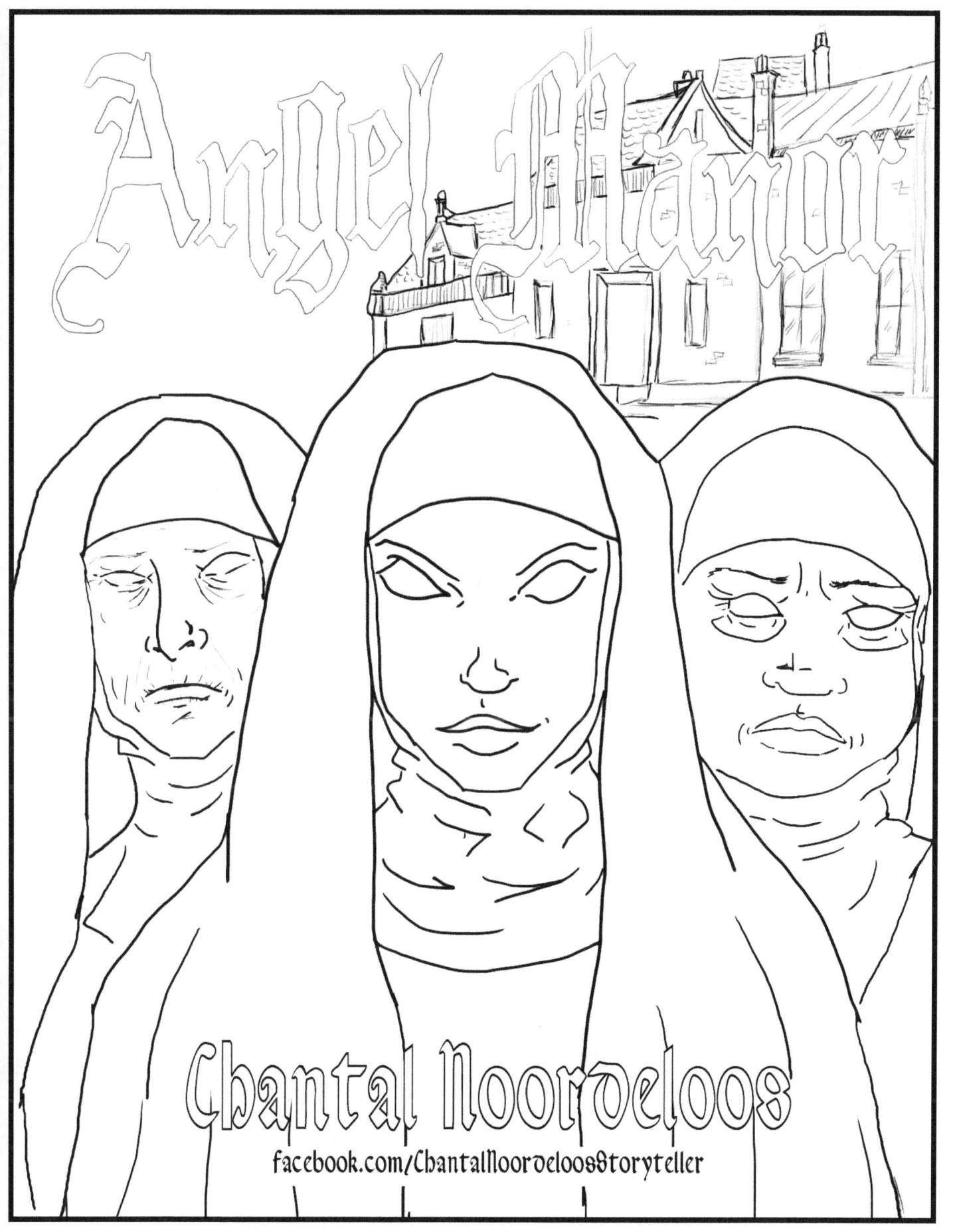

KATIE

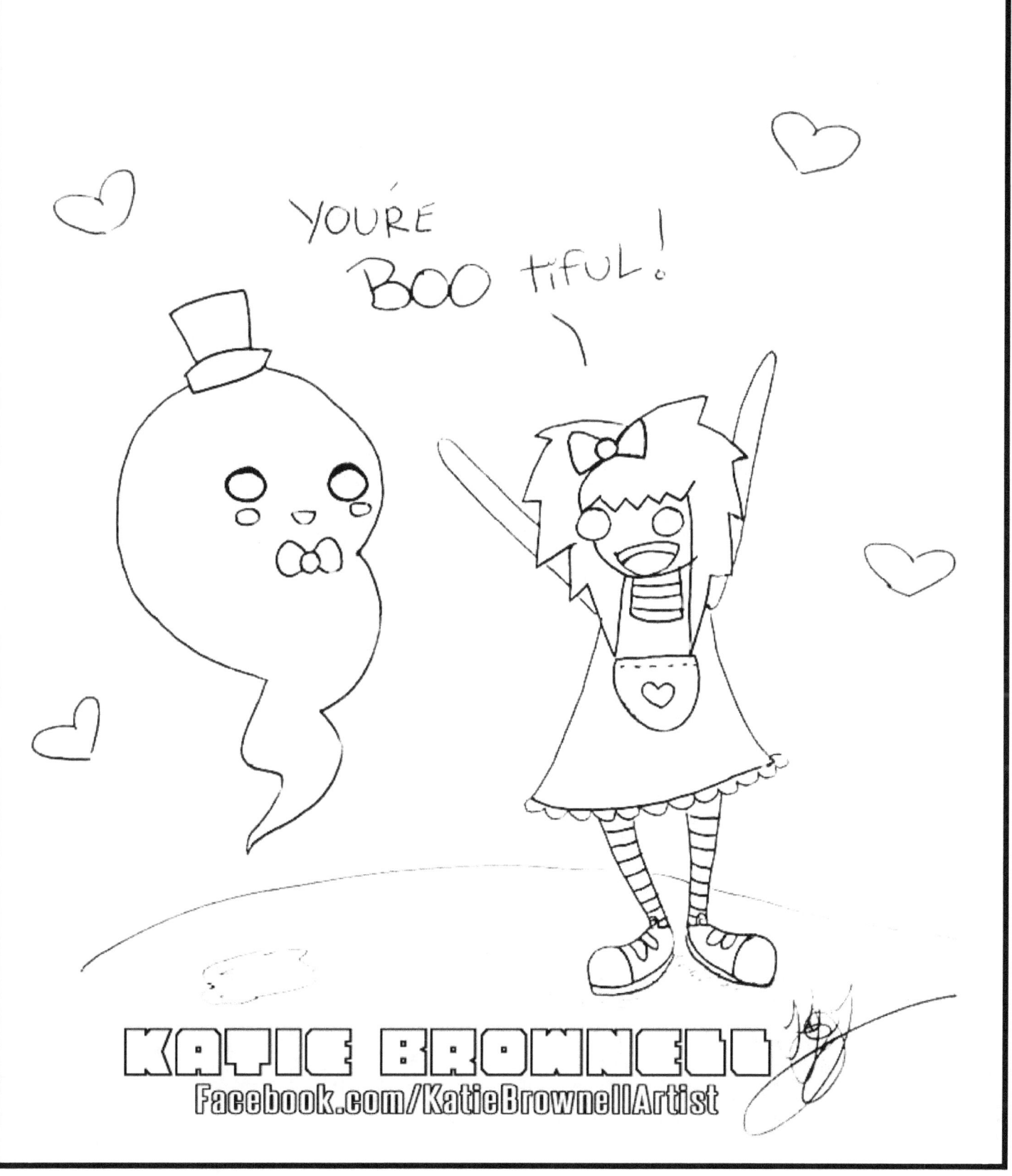

RICK

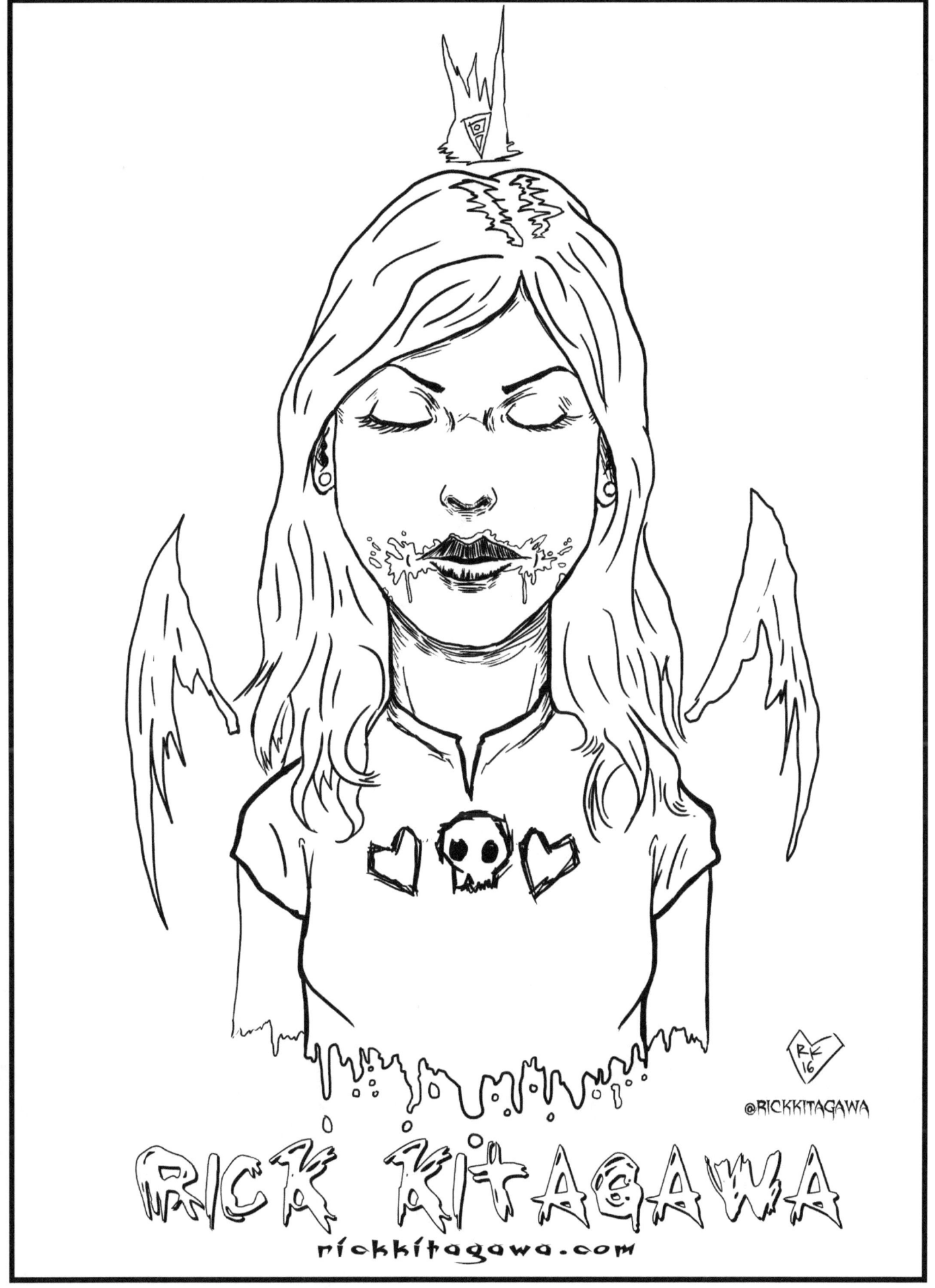

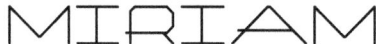

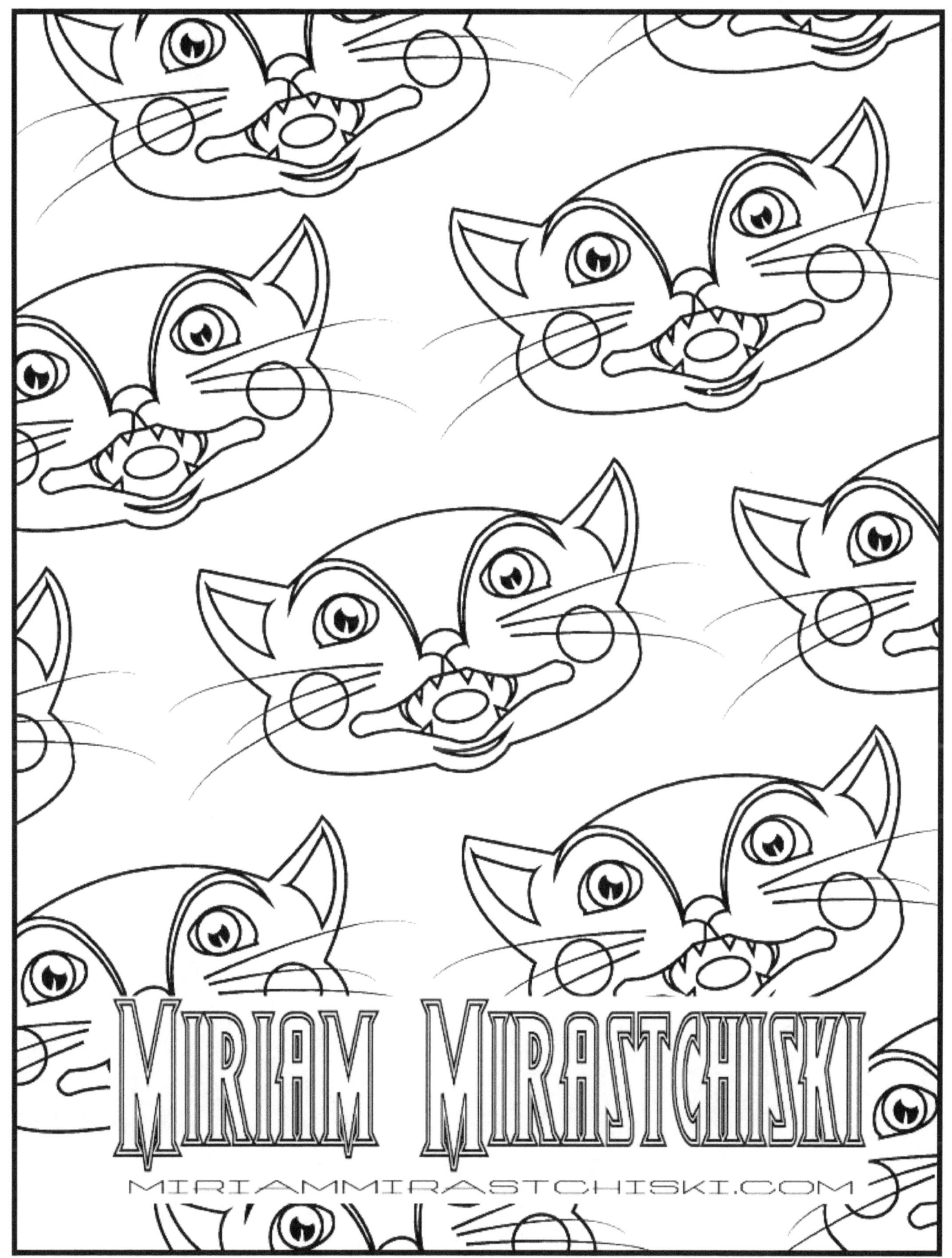

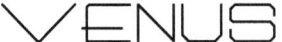

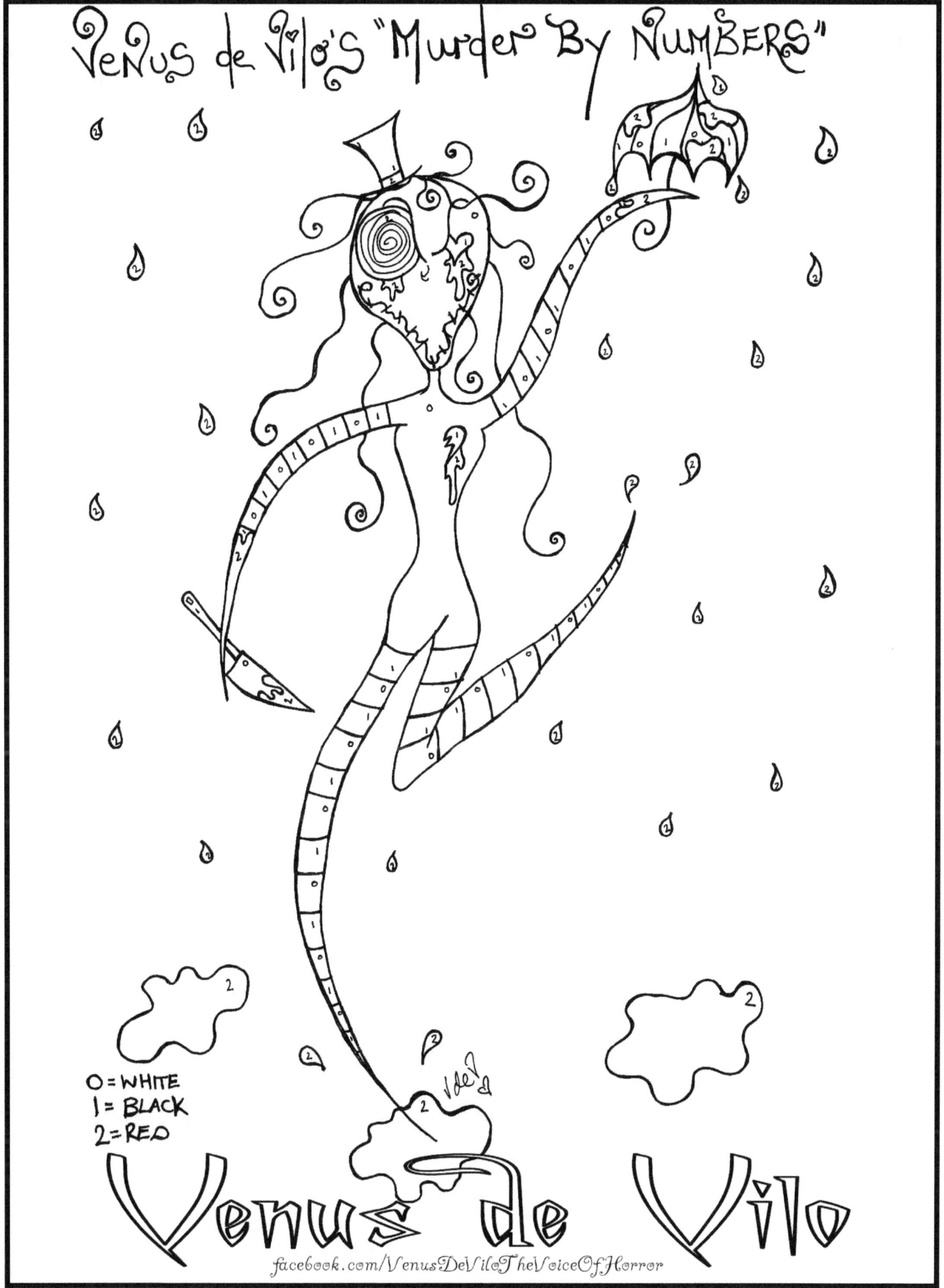

THANK YOU FOR JOINING ME ON THIS VISUAL JOURNEY

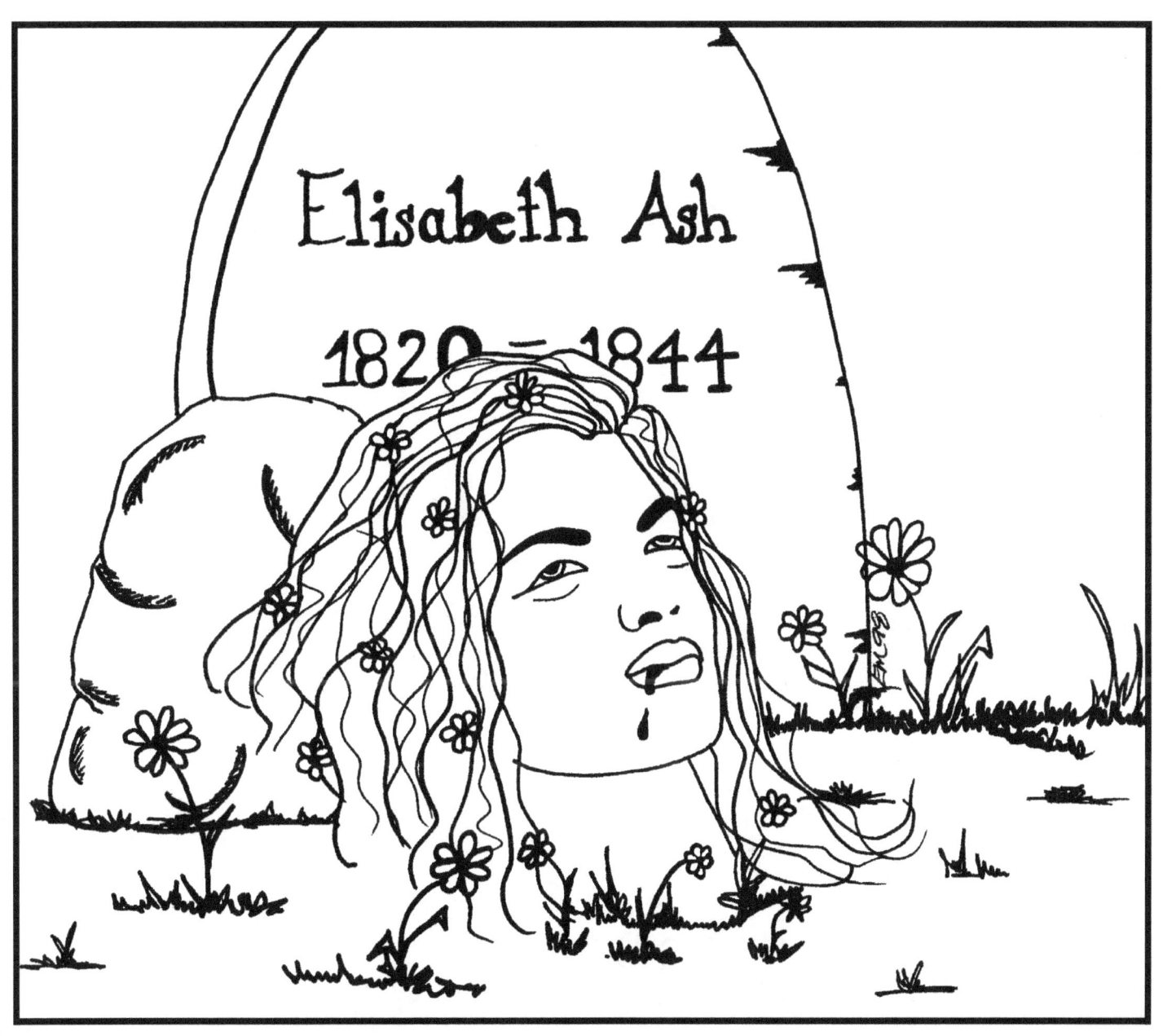

www.ingramcontent.com/pod-product-compliance
Lightning Source LLC
Chambersburg PA
CBHW080714190526
45169CB00006B/2371